What Readers Are Saying About
Seeing the Unseen

"For over fifty years, my wheelchair has helped me focus on eternal things, rather than the passing things of this earth. But how do you set your mind on heavenly realities? How can we live, knowing that everything we do on earth has a direct bearing on our eternal estate? My friend Randy Alcorn answers these questions on every page of his wonderful new book, *Seeing the Unseen*. I highly recommend this ninety-day devotional to all Christians who want to enrich their joy in Heaven!"

—JONI EARECKSON TADA, founder of Joni and Friends International Disability Center

"Alcorn's insights from the Scriptures are clear, cogent, profound, and practical. We all need to be reminded of the hope we have in Christ. I highly recommend this excellent compilation of Alcorn's finest thoughts on Heaven and living for eternity."

—DR. DAVID P. CRAIG, lead pastor at Valley Baptist Church, San Rafael, CA

"This devotional written by Randy Alcorn is one of the best I have read or own. Topics are all spot on, and scripture accompanies each devotional. Many have brought great encouragement to me, and many more have brought great conviction. Be good to yourself and read this daily devotional."

—Jean

"This is like sitting down in the study of a trusted pastor for a daily talk."

—Amazon Customer

"Like all of Randy Alcorn's writing, it's a refreshing drink of eternity for my day!"

—M. G.

SEEING
the
UNSEEN

Books by Randy Alcorn

EXPANDED EDITION

SEEING
the
UNSEEN

**A 90-Day Devotional
to Set Your Mind on Eternity**

RANDY
ALCORN

MULTNOMAH

SEEING THE UNSEEN

Hardcover ISBN 978-0-7352-9079-2
eBook ISBN 978-0-7352-9080-8

Library of Congress Cataloging-in-Publication Data
Names: Alcorn, Randy C., author.
Title: Seeing the unseen: a ninety-day devotional to set your mind on eternity / Randy Alcorn.
Description: Expanded edition. | Colorado Springs : Multnomah, [2017] | Includes bibliographical references.
Identifiers: LCCN 2017025304| ISBN 9780735290792 (hardcover) | ISBN 9780735290808 (electronic)
Subjects: LCSH: Meditations. | Eternity—Meditations. | Future life—Christianity—Meditations.
Classification: LCC BV4832.3 .A43 2017 | DDC 242—dc23 LC record available at https://lccn.loc.gov/2017025304

Printed in the United States of America
2017—First Multnomah Edition

10 9 8 7 6 5 4 3 2 1

Many thanks to Stephanie Anderson,
who helped compile and assemble my
writings in this book,
and to Doreen Button, Laura Barker, Pam
Shoup, and Holly Briscoe,
all of whom played important parts in the editing.

Contents

Fixing Our Eyes
on the Unseen

D o you have a life verse? Mine is 2 Corinthians 4:18, which is posted on our ministry website and at the end of every e-mail I send:

> So we fix our eyes not on what is seen, but on what is unseen.
> For what is seen is temporary, but what is unseen is eternal. (NIV)

What does Scripture mean when it tells us to fix our eyes on what we can't even see? How do we begin to do that?

Even though as Christians we affirm the reality of the spiritual realm, sometimes we succumb to the naturalistic assumption that what we see is real and what we don't see isn't. Many people conclude that God can't be real because we can't see Him. And Heaven can't be real because we can't see it. But we must recognize our blindness. The blind must take by faith that there are stars in the sky. If they depend on their ability to see, they will conclude there are no stars.

For many people, including many believers, Heaven is a mysterious word describing a place they don't understand and therefore don't look forward to. We will one day be delivered from the blindness that obscures the light of God's world. In the meantime, here in what C. S. Lewis called the Shadowlands, we must remind ourselves what Scripture tells us about the life to come. What we otherwise could not have known about Heaven, "God has revealed to us through the Spirit" (1 Corinthians 2:10). God tells us about our eternal home in His Word, not so we can shrug our shoulders and remain ignorant, but because He wants us to anticipate what awaits us and those we love, and because it has the power to transform the way we live today.

Life on Earth matters, not because it's the only life we have but precisely because it isn't—it's the beginning of a life that will continue without end. It's the precursor of life on the New Earth. Eternal life doesn't begin when we die; it has already begun. With eternity in view, nearly any honest activity—whether building a shed, driving a bus, pruning trees, changing diapers, or caring for a patient—can be an investment in God's kingdom.

God is eternal. His Place is eternal. His Word is eternal. His people are eternal. Center your life around God, His Place, His Word, and His people, and reach out to those eternal souls who desperately long for His person and His place. Then no matter what you do for a living, your days here will make a profound difference for eternity and you will be fulfilling the biblical admonition to fix your eyes on what is unseen.

This book includes ninety daily devotionals on a variety of topics related to living each day purposefully with an eternal perspective. I hope these readings will encourage you to live with eternity in mind as you follow Jesus with all your heart.

Randy Alcorn

Living for the Line

When we live with eternity in view, even the tasks of washing dishes and mowing lawns become an investment in God's plan.

The people who change lives are the ones who point us away from the world's short-term perspective to God's long-term perspective. Life on Earth is a dot, a brief window of opportunity; life in Heaven (and ultimately on the New Earth) is a line going out from that dot for eternity. If we're smart, we'll live not for the dot but for the line.

When we view our short today in light of eternity's long tomorrow (to use A. W. Tozer's expression), even the little choices we make become tremendously important. After death we will never have another chance to share Christ with one who can be saved, to give a cup of water to the thirsty, to serve our church. No wonder Scripture commands us, "Set your minds on things above, not on earthly things" (Colossians 3:2, NIV).

From childhood most of us learn to stifle our thirst for the eternal, replacing it with the pursuit of the temporal. But when we live with eternity in view, we'll do everything with a transformed perspective, not only preaching and witnessing but also washing dishes and mowing lawns. Almost any honest activity can be an eternal contribution, an investment in God's eternal plan.

Perspectives from God's Word

"And whatever you do, in word or deed, do everything in the name of the Lord Jesus, giving thanks to God the Father through him" (Colossians 3:17).

"And whoever gives one of these little ones even a cup of cold water because he is a disciple, truly, I say to you, he will by no means lose his reward" (Matthew 10:42).

Perspectives from God's People

"Let no one apologize for the powerful emphasis Christianity lays upon the doctrine of the world to come. Right there lies its immense superiority to everything else within the whole sphere of human thought or experience. . . . We do well to think of the long tomorrow." —A. W. Tozer

"If you read history you will find that the Christians who did most for the present world were precisely those who thought most of the next." —C. S. Lewis

For more: Read the blog post "Six Eternal Truths to Remember Each Day": epm.org/6truths

Seeing God
as the Source

We should see God as the Source of all good and our Sustainer through everything bad. God alone is the Fountain of Life.

As Romans 1:20 suggests, God's fingerprints can be seen everywhere in His creation: on the friendships we enjoy, the food we eat, and the pleasures of family, work, and hobbies. But we should never let these secondary pleasures eclipse our love for God. In fact, sometimes we must forgo them to focus more fully on Him. We should thank Him for all of life's joys and allow them to draw us closer to Him.

God welcomes prayers of thanksgiving for a simple meal, a lively conversation, a captivating book, and every other good thing. When we fail to acknowledge God as the Source of all good things, we fail to give Him the recognition and glory He deserves. We separate God from joy, which is like trying to separate heat from fire or wetness from rain.

God is the Source of all good and our Sustainer through everything bad. Consider the perspective of one accustomed to suffering who can still say, "They feast on the abundance of your house, and you give them drink from the river of your delights. For with you is the fountain of life" (Psalm 36:8–9). God alone is the Fountain of Life. Without Him there could be neither life nor joy, neither abundance nor delights.

Perspectives from God's Word

"My heart exults, and with my song I give thanks to him" (Psalm 28:7).

"Every good gift and every perfect gift is from above" (James 1:17).

Perspectives from God's People

"There are but two lessons for Christians to learn: the one is, to enjoy God in every thing; the other is, to enjoy every thing in God." —Charles Simeon

"He loves Thee too little who loves anything together with Thee, which he loves not for Thy sake." —Augustine

For more: Read the blog post "Longing for God and Joy, from Augustine": epm.org/longingjoy

The Preserving Power of Humility

When we become proud, we operate outside the grace God gives only to the humble. Humility preserves us; pride destroys us.

When we start thinking we're special, that we deserve everyone's respect, that we have a lot to offer, then we become proud. That means God is opposed to us, and we are operating outside of the grace that He gives only to the humble. We become a fall waiting to happen: "Pride goes before destruction, and a haughty spirit before a fall" (Proverbs 16:18).

Humility preserves us; pride destroys us. Acting in arrogance is like wearing a sign that says "Kick me." Being proud is a prayer to God: "Strike me down." It's a prayer He's certain to answer. Every day, every hour, we choose either to humble ourselves or to be proud.

If you want to be humble, take a good look at God and then a good look at yourself, and notice the difference. When you see Him as He is and yourself as you are, the very thought of being proud or arrogant should be absolutely laughable.

Perspectives from God's Word

"Whoever exalts himself will be humbled, and whoever humbles himself will be exalted" (Matthew 23:12).

"You who are younger, be subject to the elders. Clothe yourselves, all of you, with humility toward one another, for 'God opposes the proud but gives grace to the humble.' Humble yourselves, therefore, under the mighty hand of God so that at the proper time he may exalt you" (1 Peter 5:5–6).

Perspectives from God's People

"Pride is spiritual cancer: it eats up the very possibility of love, or contentment, or even common sense." —C. S. Lewis

"They that know God will be humble; they that know themselves cannot be proud." —John Flavel

For more: Read the blog post "Humility: Recognizing Who We Really Are": epm.org/humility

True Happiness

*When we believe ultimate happiness
is found only in God, then we will shut
out distractions and open His Word.*

If we buy into the lie that happiness is to be found in wealth, beauty, fame, or any number of endless pursuits besides Christ, we're doomed to unhappiness because we're pursuing the wrong things.

But when we believe that ultimate happiness and transcendent joy are to be found only in God, then we will, for a time, turn off all our screens—all texts and social media and movies and TV— and open the Word of God, asking His Spirit to speak joy into our lives.

It takes discipline and conscious effort to keep the Lord front and center and to find happiness in Him. But when we do, the payoff is huge.

Perspectives from God's Word

"You satisfy me more than the richest feast. I will praise you with songs of joy" (Psalm 63:5, NLT).

"Behold, I long for your precepts; in your righteousness give me life!" (Psalm 119:40).

Perspectives from God's People

"To be truly happy *a man must have sources of gladness which are not dependent on anything in this world.*"
—J. C. Ryle

"If you hope for happiness in the world, hope for it from God, and not from the world." —David Brainerd

For more: Read the blog post "Longing for Happiness: Perspectives from Blaise Pascal": epm.org/happinesspascal

Only One Way

*If we want to arrive in Heaven, we cannot
go through Buddha, Muhammad, or
Moses. We can only go through Jesus.*

Y ou may be troubled, feeling apprehensive about what awaits
you after death. Make sure of your relationship with Jesus
Christ. Be confident that you trust Him alone to save you—not
anyone or anything else, and certainly not any good works you've
done.

Jesus didn't say "I am *a* way and *a* truth and *a* life; I'm *one of
the ways* to come to the Father." He said, "I am THE way, and the
truth, and the life. No one comes to the Father except through me"
(John 14:6).

Anyone wishing to fly from Portland, Oregon, to North Caro-
lina can get there a number of ways. We can fly through Denver,
Minneapolis, Chicago, Detroit, Salt Lake City, Dallas, or Atlanta.
But if you and I want to arrive in Heaven—and we certainly should
want that—we cannot go through Buddha, Muhammad, or Moses.
We can only go through Jesus.

Perspectives from God's Word

"There is salvation in no one else, for there is no other
name under heaven given among men by which we must
be saved" (Acts 4:12).

"Behold, now is the favorable time; behold, now is the day of salvation" (2 Corinthians 6:2).

Perspectives from God's People

"The essence of sin is man substituting himself for God, while the essence of salvation is God substituting himself for man." —John Stott

"Fallen man is not simply an imperfect creature who needs improvement: he is a rebel who must lay down his arms." —C. S. Lewis

For more: Read the blog post "American Evangelicals Believe There Are Different Ways to Heaven": epm.org/differentways

The Freedom of Fearing God

Once our sins are confessed, though we still fear God, we can come boldly before His throne.

Scripture is full of commands to fear God, and it is also full of commands not to be afraid. If we fear God, we need not be afraid of anyone or anything else. But if we don't fear God, we have reason to be afraid of other things. We fear God when we come to grips with the fact that He is always right and we are not, that He is in charge and we are not: "Fear God and keep his commandments, for this is the whole duty of man" (Ecclesiastes 12:13).

God is not a genie, under our control. He is the Master. In a culture that so values independence and self-determination, it's not easy to accept our calling to be a servant. Christ is in charge of the universe whether or not we recognize Him—but when we do, we honor Him by submitting to His lordship.

In many Scripture passages, God calls upon us to fear Him. But once our sins are confessed, He tells us in Romans 8:15 that we can come to Him saying, "Abba! Father!" (meaning "Papa" or "Daddy"). We are welcome to go boldly before His throne with the access permitted only to the King's children. We still fear Him but in a way that does not diminish our love for Him or His for us.

"Let us then with confidence draw near to the throne of grace" (Hebrews 4:16).

Perspectives from God's Word

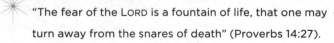

"The fear of the LORD is a fountain of life, that one may turn away from the snares of death" (Proverbs 14:27).

"Fear the LORD and serve him faithfully with all your heart. For consider what great things he has done for you" (1 Samuel 12:24).

Perspectives from God's People

"The fear of God is the death of every other fear. Like a mighty lion, it chases all other fears before it." —Charles Spurgeon

"We are more concerned about looking stupid (fear of people) *than we are about acting sinfully* (fear of the Lord)." —Edward T. Welch

For more: Read the blog post "The Fear of God": epm.org/feargod

He Is Always Sovereign

Is God sovereign only when we get our way, or is He always sovereign? The God who's sovereign in small things also controls the big ones.

The One in control of the universe has His time and place for all of us. Knowing this should help us walk by faith as we seek His face about what to do and where to go next. He is sovereign, never taken by surprise. He is the God of providence who raises up not just Esther but each of us for "such a time as this" (Esther 4:14).

The true test of our belief in a sovereign God is when we have a week of rain on a long-awaited camping trip, or the washer—with our best delicate clothes in it—fills with muddy water from a broken water main. (This happened to my wife, Nanci.) Is God sovereign when He deals with the rise and fall of empires but not when my tent leaks or my favorite shirt is ruined? Is He always sovereign or just when I get my way?

I hope you have a big view of God and His sovereignty. He is the God of all greatness. Don't underestimate Him.

Perspectives from God's Word

"For I am God, and there is no other; I am God, and there is none like me" (Isaiah 46:9).

"Now to him who is able to do far more abundantly than all that we ask or think, according to the power at work within us, to him be glory in the church and in Christ Jesus throughout all generations, forever and ever. Amen" (Ephesians 3:20–21).

Perspectives from God's People

"The sovereignty of God is the one impregnable rock to which the suffering human heart must cling. The circumstances surrounding our lives are no accident: they may be the work of evil, but that evil is held firmly within the mighty hand of our sovereign God." —Margaret Clarkson

"Most Christians salute the sovereignty of God but believe in the sovereignty of man." —R. C. Sproul

For more: Watch the video "Difficult Truths & Deep Love: Pondering Sovereignty, Suffering, and the Promise of Heaven": epm.org/deeplove

The Grace of Giving

Jesus Christ is the matchless Giver.
No matter how much we give,
we can never outgive God.

When God provides more money, we often think, *This is a blessing.* Yes, but it would be just as scriptural to say, "This is a test." Abundance isn't God's provision for me to live in luxury. God entrusts me with His money not to build my kingdom on Earth but to build His kingdom in Heaven.

The act of giving is a vivid reminder that it's all about God, not about us. It's saying we are not the point; He is the point. He does not exist for us; we exist for Him. God's money has a higher purpose than our affluence. Giving affirms Christ's lordship; it dethrones us and exalts Him.

As we learn to give, we draw closer to God. But no matter how far we move along in the grace of giving, Jesus Christ remains the matchless Giver: "For you know the grace of our Lord Jesus Christ, that though he was rich, yet for your sakes he became poor, so that you through his poverty might become rich" (2 Corinthians 8:9, NIV). "Rich" in this sense is not about finances, and this is not the health and wealth gospel; God gives to us in a thousand ways besides material prosperity. No matter how much we give, we can never outgive God.

Perspectives from God's Word

"You will be enriched in every way so that you can be generous on every occasion" (2 Corinthians 9:11, NIV).

"Everything comes from you, and we have given you only what comes from your hand" (1 Chronicles 29:14, NIV).

Perspectives from God's People

"I shovel out the money, and God shovels it back—but God has a bigger shovel." —R. G. LeTourneau

"There ought to be things we should like to do and cannot do because our charities expenditure excludes them." —C. S. Lewis

For more: Read the article "31 Radical, Liberating Questions to Ask God About Your Giving": epm.org/31questions

Grasping Our Need for Grace

*When we fail to see that we have
sinned against God above all,
we will inevitably minimize our sin.*

The better we understand our sinfulness and alienation from God, the more we appreciate God's grace. Charles Spurgeon put it this way: "Too many think lightly of sin, and therefore think lightly of the Saviour."[1]

When we fail to see that we have sinned against God above all, the One who has maximum worthiness, then no matter how bad we feel about what we've done to others, we will inevitably minimize our sin.

We try to explain away sin in terms of "That's not what I meant" or "I did what my father always did to me" or "I wouldn't have done this if you hadn't done that." All these statements minimize our evil and thereby minimize the greatness of God's grace in atoning for it.

Perspectives from God's Word

"Against you, you only, have I sinned and done what is evil in your sight, so that you may be justified in your words and blameless in your judgment" (Psalm 51:4).

"Whoever conceals his transgressions will not prosper, but he who confesses and forsakes them will obtain mercy" (Proverbs 28:13).

Perspectives from God's People

"The thing that awakens the deepest well of gratitude in a human being is that God has forgiven sin." —Oswald Chambers

"The beginning of the way to heaven, is to feel that we are on the way to hell." —J. C. Ryle

For more: Read the blog post "The Cross of Christ: A Symbol Not of Our Worthiness, but Our Unworthiness": epm.org/symbolcross

Homesick for Heaven

*What we really want is the Person we were
made for—Jesus—and the place we were
made for—Heaven. Nothing less will satisfy.*

When I travel, I find particular joy in those places that remind me of my lifelong home in Oregon. Likewise, one of the greatest joys that Christian pilgrims find in this world is in those moments when it reminds them of Heaven, their true home they've read about and dreamed of. They live with the exhilarating assurance that at this very moment their beloved Savior is making it ready for them.

The Bible tells us we are pilgrims, strangers, aliens, and ambassadors working far from home (see Ephesians 2:19; 2 Corinthians 5:20; Hebrews 11:13–16). Our citizenship is in Heaven. But often we've become so attached to this world that we live for the wrong kingdom. We forget our true home, built for us by our Bridegroom.

Nothing is more often misdiagnosed than our homesickness for Heaven. We think that what we want is money, sex, drugs, alcohol, a new job, a raise, a doctorate, a spouse, a large-screen television, a new car, a vacation. What we really want is the Person we were made for, Jesus, and the place we were made for, Heaven. Nothing less can satisfy us. "Your name and renown are the desire of our hearts" (Isaiah 26:8, NIV).

Perspectives from God's Word

"In my Father's house are many rooms. If it were not so, would I have told you that I go to prepare a place for you? And if I go and prepare a place for you, I will come again and will take you to myself, that where I am you may be also" (John 14:2–3).

"My desire is to depart and be with Christ, for that is far better" (Philippians 1:23).

Perspectives from God's People

"To come to Thee is to come home from exile, to come to land out of the raging storm, to come to rest after long labour, to come to the goal of my desires and the summit of my wishes." —Charles Spurgeon

"If I find in myself a desire which no experience in this world can satisfy, the most probable explanation is that I was made for another world." —C. S. Lewis

For more: Watch the video "Homesick for Heaven": epm.org/homesick

Putting God's Word First

Examine truth-claims against God's Word. Reject what doesn't sync. Don't let social media and news feeds forge your worldview.

We should come to God's Word to examine truth-claims. If we're more eager to watch reality TV, sports, or the news than we are to read God's Word, inevitably our worldview will be influenced more by television than by God. How could it be otherwise?

As biblical Christians, we must not only affirm the inspiration of God's Word; we must also consciously critique everything else in light of Scripture. Otherwise we will unconsciously conform our minds to the world, the flesh, and the devil. We must seek to continually evaluate our beliefs and lifestyle preferences by God's Word.

As the old adage says, "If you always do what you've always done, you'll always get what you've always got." Our hearts and characters won't change unless our daily habits change. Holy habits such as meditation, prayer, and church attendance should be determined commitments. How we spend our time verifies what we value most: TV, the Internet, or God's Word. The fruit of the Spirit includes self-control (see Galatians 5:22–23). We already know what the world thinks; how much more do we need to hear? Let's choose to be in touch with the mind of God.

Perspectives from God's Word

"The Bereans [Jews] were of more noble character than the Thessalonians, for they received the message with great eagerness and examined the Scriptures every day to see if what Paul said was true" (Acts 17:11, NIV).

"Let the word of Christ dwell in you richly" (Colossians 3:16).

Perspectives from God's People

"The new life in Christ . . . must be nourished. . . . This is possible only in communion with Christ . . . and through the word of Scripture." —Herman Bavinck

"The vigor of our spiritual life will be in exact proportion to the place held by the Bible in our life and thoughts." —George Müller

For more: Read the blog post "Investing Time in Reading's God's Word": epm.org/investingtime

A Demonstration of Matchless Love

God could have created us without loving us, but He would not have gone to the Cross without loving us.

Christian love finds its pattern and origin in God. God loves us even though we are unlovable. God loves us even though we don't deserve it. We haven't earned His love. We are unworthy. This love, expressed at the cross of Jesus, is *agape* love, unmerited and free.

Pastor Colin S. Smith writes, "When our sin reached its full horror, God's love was displayed in all its glory. If you doubt God's love for you, look at the cross. No other love can match this. Nothing else in our experience can come close. God's love for us in Christ is greater than we ever dared to dream."[2]

The cross of Jesus means that God, out of love, did everything for you and for me. So why shouldn't we be willing to do anything for Him?

Perspectives from God's Word

"God shows his love for us in that while we were still sinners, Christ died for us" (Romans 5:8).

"[I pray] that you, being rooted and grounded in love, may have strength to comprehend with all the saints what is the breadth and length and height and depth, and to know the love of Christ that surpasses knowledge, that you may be filled with all the fullness of God" (Ephesians 3:17–19).

Perspectives from God's People

"Christians have learned that when there seems to be no other evidence of God's love, they cannot escape the cross." —D. A. Carson

"God does something *to* us as well as *for* us through the cross. He persuades us that He loves us." —Sinclair Ferguson

For more: Read the blog post "God's Limitless Love": epm.org/limitless

Contagious Excitement for Heaven

Like a bride's dream of sharing a home with her groom, our eager anticipation of Heaven should overflow and be contagious.

When I anticipate what my first glimpse of Heaven will be like, I remember the first time I went snorkeling. Etched in my memory is a certain sound, one that startled me several times, causing me to look all around me. Then I realized what it was: the sound of my own gasp going through the snorkel as I marveled at the sights. I imagine our first glimpse of Heaven will cause us to similarly gasp in amazement and delight. That first gasp will likely be followed by many more as we encounter new sights in that endlessly wonderful place.

Like a bride's dream of sharing a home with her groom, our eager anticipation of Heaven should be overflowing and contagious. The more I learn about God, the more excited I get about Heaven. The more I learn about Heaven, the more excited I get about God. Jesus said, "I am going there to prepare a place for you. . . . I will come back and take you to be with me that you also may be where I am" (John 14:2–3, NIV).

The hope of Heaven is the light at the end of life's tunnel. It not only makes the tunnel endurable; it fills our hearts with anticipation of the world into which we will one day emerge. Not just a better world, but a new and perfect world. A world alive, fresh, beautiful. A world devoid of pain, suffering, and war. A world without earthquakes, without tsunamis, without tragedy. A world ruled by the only One worthy of ruling.

Perspectives from God's Word

"They desire a better country, that is, a heavenly one. Therefore God is not ashamed to be called their God, for he has prepared for them a city" (Hebrews 11:16).

"You make known to me the path of life; in your presence there is fullness of joy; at your right hand are pleasures forevermore" (Psalm 16:11).

Perspectives from God's People

"When Christ calls me home, I shall go with the gladness of a boy bounding away from his school." —Adoniram Judson, on his deathbed

"Anyone who has been in foreign lands longs to return to his own native land. . . . We regard paradise as our native land." —Cyprian

For more: Read the blog post "Heavenly Minded and of Earthly Good": epm.org/earthlygood

Forgiveness Is a Choice

Forgiveness is a matter of choice, not feelings. We demonstrate true forgiveness when we refuse to brood over the sins committed against us.

The assumption that life shouldn't be so hard leads to self-pity and endless finger pointing. We see our circumstances as unfair and ourselves as victims, and we focus on the offenses others have committed against us. We fail to realize that those offenses pale in comparison to our own offenses against God, who not only forgives us but requires and enables us to forgive others and then move forward, free from the past.

Forgiveness is a matter of choice, not feelings. Yes, we may remember the facts, but we must not allow ourselves to dwell on them. It is possible to "forgive and forget" if we truly do forgive. But we will never forget what we choose to brood over, demonstrating that we haven't truly forgiven.

C. S. Lewis wrote, "To be a Christian means to forgive the inexcusable, because God has forgiven the inexcusable in you."[3] Jesus said if your brother "sins against you seven times in the day, and turns to you seven times, saying, 'I repent,' you must forgive him" (Luke 17:4). Forgiveness is not unrealistic, and yes, sometimes we must exercise tough love and take strong corrective steps in relationships. Yet all the while we must refuse to rehearse and dwell on the offenses of others.

Perspectives from God's Word

"If you forgive others their trespasses, your heavenly Father will also forgive you, but if you do not forgive others their trespasses, neither will your Father forgive your trespasses" (Matthew 6:14–15).

"Be kind to one another, tenderhearted, forgiving one another, as God in Christ forgave you" (Ephesians 4:32).

Perspectives from God's People

"As Christians we are forgiven people. We are likewise called to be forgiving people." —R. C. Sproul

"It takes two to reconcile, so it is not always possible to be reconciled. But it takes only one to forgive. So if people do us wrong, we should forgive them, whether or not they ask for forgiveness. We cannot cancel their sin. Only God can do that, and he will only do it if they repent. But what we can do is set aside our own anger, bitterness, and resentment towards them." —Philip Graham Ryken

For more: Read the article "Good News: God Forgives": epm.org/forgiveness

The Happiness of Studying God's Word

When we're right with God, we're delighted with His words, because in them we see His majesty, His beauty, and His happiness.

Happiness among believers is proportionate to the time invested in the humble study of God's Word. There's nothing wrong with learning about sports and politics. But only God's Word prepares us to live wisely and to die well.

Joni Eareckson Tada says, "Great faith . . . [is] simply taking God at His word and taking the next step."⁴ Just as we can't follow signs without getting on the road, we can't take God at His Word unless we spend time reading, hearing, and contemplating it.

Through Scripture meditation, prayer, group Bible study, and sitting under the teaching of God's Word, we get to know our Lord better and draw closer to Him. In the process, we cultivate overflowing happiness. People are unhappy because they listen to the thousands of unhappy voices, including much media, that clamor for their attention. Joy comes from hearing and believing words from the Source of joy.

Perspectives from God's Word

"The laws of the LORD are true; each one is fair. They are more desirable than gold, even the finest gold. They are

sweeter than honey, even honey dripping from the comb"
(Psalm 19:9–10, NLT).

"As your words came to me I drank them in, and they filled
my heart with joy and happiness because I belong to you,
O LORD, the God who rules over all" (Jeremiah 15:16, NET).

Perspectives from God's People

"There is no true or solid peace to be enjoyed in the world
except in the way of reposing upon the promises of God."
—John Calvin

"A growing chorus of joyous voices round the world fairly
sing that spending their hours with God is the most thrilling
joy ever known. . . . Spending time with the Lord is not a
grim duty." —Frank Laubach

For more: Read the blog post "Seeking to Be Happy in Christ: My Interview
with Bible Gateway": epm.org/seekinghappy

The Master Artist

*Eden has been trampled. Nevertheless,
in nature and art and music we see and hear
vestiges of God's beauty and creativity.*

To study creation is to study the Creator. Science should be worshipful discovery because the heavens and all creation declare God's glory (see Psalm 19:1). God reveals His creative genius in flowers, waterfalls, animals, and planets. God's character is written large in nature in His organization, skill, precision, and attention to detail. He's the Master Artist.

Cosmic rays are highly energetic particles that flow into our solar system from deep in outer space, but where do they actually come from? It's been a mystery for fifty years. This mystery and countless others have not so much frustrated scientists as fascinated them. Watch their interviews and read their articles; their wonder about things they don't comprehend is palpable. You don't have to be able to wrap your mind around something in order to see its beauty.

We're told that God's "invisible qualities" can be "clearly seen" in "what has been made" (Romans 1:20, NIV). This is God's general revelation. Eden has been trampled, torched, savaged, and abandoned. Nevertheless, in our own bodies and in our world we can see the intricacy of God's craftsmanship; and in flowers and rain and art and music we see and hear vestiges of God's beauty and creativity.

Perspectives from God's Word

"God saw everything that he had made, and behold, it was very good" (Genesis 1:31).

"Yours is the day, yours also the night; you have established the heavenly lights and the sun. You have fixed all the boundaries of the earth; you have made summer and winter" (Psalm 74:16–17).

Perspectives from God's People

"As a house implies a builder, and a garment a weaver, and a door a carpenter, so does the existence of the Universe imply a Creator." —Marquis de Vauvenargues

"The more I study nature, the more I stand amazed at the work of the Creator." —Louis Pasteur

For more: Read the blog post "Psalm 19: God's General and Special Revelation": epm.org/psalm19

Separated from the Source of Happiness

Your yearning for happiness is a gift from God, and He alone can ultimately satisfy you.

A dam and Eve fell away from God and happiness because of their disobedience. However, they never lost their desire to be happy. As their descendants, we inherited their separation from God and therefore from happiness. Ages later, we retain a profound awareness that we were once happy—and that we should be happy still.

This compelling desire for genuine happiness, while at times painful, is God's grace to us. Longing for the happiness humankind once knew, we can be drawn toward true happiness in Christ, which is offered us in the gospel.

Because we were made for greatness, the world's superficiality is unsatisfying. We ache for someone, somehow, to bring us lasting happiness. That someone is Jesus, and that somehow is His redemptive work.

Perspectives from God's Word

"Let them thank the LORD for his steadfast love, for his wondrous works to the children of man! For he satisfies the longing soul, and the hungry soul he fills with good things" (Psalm 107:8–9).

"Come, everyone who thirsts, come to the waters; and he who has no money, come, buy and eat! Come, buy wine and milk without money and without price" (Isaiah 55:1).

Perspectives from God's People

"What else does this longing and helplessness proclaim, but that there was once in each person a true happiness, of which all that now remains is the empty print and trace? . . . This infinite abyss can only be filled with something that is infinite and unchanging—in other words, by God himself."
—Blaise Pascal

"Certainly by sinning we lost both piety and happiness; but when we lost happiness, we did not lose the love of it."
—Augustine

For more: Read the article "Why Do We Long for Happiness? (Chapter 1 of Happiness by Randy Alcorn)": epm.org/longhappiness

Listening to His Voice

*Time spent in God's Word and
prayer is never wasted; it sets
our heart's compass to true north.*

M y sheep listen to my voice," Jesus said (John 10:27, NIV).
Have you been listening to His voice lately? Have you been
putting your ear to His Word and asking Him to speak to you?

I enjoy regular time with God. Some of my sweetest memories
are of days dedicated wholly to Him: having meals with just Him,
taking a long bike ride with Him, talking with Him, reading good
books with Him by my side, listening to His Word, and asking
Him to speak to me.

There is no substitute for time spent with our Father in Heaven.
Time spent in His Word and prayer is never wasted. It turns our
heart's compass to true north and sets the tone for all our activities
and interactions.

Perspectives from God's Word

"'You will seek me and find me, when you seek me with all
your heart . . . ,' declares the LORD" (Jeremiah 29:13–14).

"With my whole heart I seek you; let me not wander from
your commandments!" (Psalm 119:10).

Perspectives from God's People

"We rise from the Bible . . . with a knowledge of the character of God. There is a real analogy here to our relation with an earthly friend. How do we come to know one another? Not all at once, but by years of observation of one another's actions. . . . So it is, somewhat, with the knowledge of God that we óbtain from the Bible. . . . By what we see we learn to know Him." —J. Gresham Machen

"One gem from that ocean is worth all the pebbles from earthly streams." —Robert Murray M'Cheyne, *speaking of the Scriptures*

For more: Read the blog post "Longing for God and Hearing His Voice, from A. W. Tozer": epm.org/voice

Seeking God's Will

The Bible is the revealed will of God. If you want to live in His will, then "Let the word of Christ dwell in you richly" (Colossians 3:16).

Knowing the will of God has become much easier for me as years pass. It's not that I have to know exactly where to go, but that I ask Him for direction and insight, seek to surrender each day to Him, and ask Him to bring into my life those divine appointments that make life so interesting. God appoints the times and places we live (see Acts 17:26), and He is a Master of exact timing.

The Bible is the revealed will of God. If you want to live in His will, then "let the word of Christ dwell in you richly" (Colossians 3:16). Fill your heart and mind with the Word of God, trust in His empowerment to obey Him, and confess and repent when you disobey and fail. If you do this, you will be living in the will of God.

God's will is more than a duty; it's a joyful opportunity. What a privilege to serve Him! I want to know Christ, like Paul said in Philippians 3. When we know Christ, when we fellowship with His people, and when we saturate ourselves in His Word, knowing God's will becomes less mysterious, and doing His will tends to follow naturally (or supernaturally, depending on how you look at it).

Perspectives from God's Word

"May the God of peace . . . equip you with everything good that you may do his will, working in us that which is pleasing in his sight, through Jesus Christ" (Hebrews 13:20–21).

"Do not be conformed to this world, but be transformed by the renewal of your mind, that by testing you may discern what is the will of God" (Romans 12:2).

Perspectives from God's People

"Let us pray to the Lord that we may do his will on earth as it is done in heaven; that is, *joyfully, without the slightest weariness.* When our hearts are right, it is a glad thing to serve God, though it be only to unloose the latchets [laces] of our Master's shoes." —Charles Spurgeon

"There are only two kinds of people in the end: those who say to God, 'Thy will be done,' and those to whom God says, in the end, '*Thy* will be done.'" —C. S. Lewis

For more: Read the blog post "Knowing God's Will": epm.org/godswill

True Repentance

*To be repentant means to be committed
to doing whatever is necessary to
keep from falling back into sin.*

Repentance is more than reciting well-calculated words while trying to minimize our losses. Genuine repentance is utterly vulnerable. It confesses more than has been found out. It never withholds information in the hope of preserving an image or a reputation. It puts itself at the mercy of others; it does not presume to direct or control them.

Psalm 51 is an expression of pure repentance. Notice there is no explanation of the extenuating circumstances—of how busy King David is, how lonely the man at the top is, how irresponsible it is for Bathsheba to be bathing in sight of the palace, how Uriah is a neglectful husband. David doesn't rationalize or justify or qualify his sin. He owns up to it, 100 percent. He simply admits he is wrong.

To be repentant means to be committed to doing whatever is necessary to keep from falling back into sin. God says through John the Baptist, "Bear fruit in keeping with repentance" (Matthew 3:8). The sincerity of our repentance is demonstrated by how willing we are to take the steps necessary to nourish our souls and reprogram our minds from the Scriptures, so we can draw on Christ's power to be righteous.

Perspectives from God's Word

"A broken and contrite heart, O God, you will not despise" (Psalm 51:17).

"Repent therefore, and turn back, that your sins may be blotted out, that times of refreshing may come from the presence of the Lord" (Acts 3:19–20).

Perspectives from God's People

"When our Lord and Master Jesus Christ said 'Repent' (Mt. 4:17), he willed the entire life of believers to be one of repentance." —Martin Luther

"The first spiritual step on the Calvary road of radical obedience to Jesus is repentance. Repentance includes remorse for inward corruption and sin. Repentance is not only remorse. It is a change of mind and heart about sin and righteousness and about Christ. It is a turning from the broken cisterns of the world to the fountain of life." —John Piper

For more: Read the article "What Is True Repentance?": epm.org/repentance

Breaking Our Addiction to Materialism

Even if materialism brought happiness in this life (which it certainly does not), it would leave us woefully unprepared for the next.

Materialism blinds us to our spiritual poverty. It's a fruitless attempt to find meaning outside of God, the Source of all life and the Giver of all good gifts. "For you say, I am rich, I have prospered, and I need nothing, not realizing that you are wretched, pitiable, poor, blind, and naked" (Revelation 3:17).

Seeking fulfillment in money, land, houses, cars, clothes, RVs, and vacations has left us bound and gagged by materialism, and like all addicts, we think our only hope lies in getting more of the same. Meanwhile, the voice of God—unheard amid the clamor—is telling us that even if materialism did bring happiness in this life (which it doesn't), it would leave us woefully unprepared for the next.

John D. Rockefeller has often been quoted as saying, "I have made many millions, but they have brought me no happiness."[5] Scripture says, "Cast but a glance at riches, and they are gone, for they will surely sprout wings and fly off to the sky like an eagle" (Proverbs 23:5, NIV). What a picture! Next time you buy a possession you long for, imagine it sprouting wings and flying off. Sooner or later it will disappear.

But if you've obeyed Jesus' words in Matthew 6:19–21 and stored up your treasures in Heaven, not on Earth, then your treasures will last forever.

Perspectives from God's Word

"[Jesus] said to them, 'Take care, and be on your guard against all covetousness, for one's life does not consist in the abundance of his possessions'" (Luke 12:15).

"Sweet is the sleep of a laborer, whether he eats little or much, but the full stomach of the rich will not let him sleep" (Ecclesiastes 5:12).

Perspectives from God's People

"Our God is a consuming fire. He consumes pride, lust, materialism, and other sin." —Leonard Ravenhill

"He is no fool who gives what he cannot keep to gain that which he cannot lose." —Jim Elliot

For more: Read the article "Materialism, Man and Morality": epm.org/materialism

The Christian Optimist

*If God is good and sits on the throne and
everything that enters our life is Father-filtered,
how can we be anything less than optimistic?*

The only proper foundation for optimism is the redemptive work of Jesus Christ. Any other foundation is sand, not rock. It will not bear the weight of our eternity.

When we build our lives on the solid foundation of Jesus' redemptive work, we can all be optimists. Even our most painful experiences in life are temporary setbacks. No Christian needs to be pessimistic.

If God is good and sits on the throne of the universe and everything that comes into our lives is Father-filtered . . . how can we be anything less than optimistic? We are in fact realists, focused on the reality that we serve a sovereign and gracious God. The Christian's optimism is based squarely on truth: God is real, the atonement is real, the resurrection is real, the Second Coming is real, God's providence is real, and the gospel really is "good news."

Perspectives from God's Word

"The LORD has become my stronghold, and my God the rock of my refuge" (Psalm 94:22).

"Since therefore the children share in flesh and blood, he himself likewise partook of the same things, that through death he might destroy the one who has the power of death, that is, the devil, and deliver all those who through fear of death were subject to lifelong slavery" (Hebrews 2:14–15).

Perspectives from God's People

"There is a difference between tears of hope and tears of hopelessness." —Erwin Lutzer

"What is your hope? Only this—His relentless grace, boundless love, patient forgiveness and unending faithfulness." —Paul Tripp

For more: Read the blog post "Biblical Optimism: The Glass That's Half Full Now Will Forever Overflow": epm.org/optimism

Coming to Grips with Our Mortality

Just as birth was our ticket to this world,
so death is our ticket to the next.
It is less of an end than a beginning.

What do we gain if we pretend mortality isn't a fact of life? It's neither morbid nor inappropriate to speak of it. Denial of truth—not truth itself—is the breeding ground for anxiety. One of the greatest gifts we can bestow on our loved ones is the honest anticipation of reunion in the better world, the one for which we were made.

Just as birth was our ticket to this world, so death is our ticket to the next. Death is less of an end than a beginning. If you were told today you would be moved from the slums to a beautiful country estate, you would not focus on the life you were ending but on the life you were beginning.

Death isn't the worst that can happen to us; on the contrary, for God's children, death leads to the best.

Perspectives from God's Word

"As it is, they desire a better country, that is, a heavenly one" (Hebrews 11:16).

"For to me to live is Christ, and to die is gain. . . . My desire
is to depart and be with Christ, for that is far better"
(Philippians 1:21, 23).

Perspectives from God's People

"Let us watch the Master's call. Let us not dread the
question—who next, and who next? Let none of us start
back as though we hoped to linger longer than others. . . .
Let us be willing to be dealt with just as our Lord pleases.
Let no doubt intervene; let no gloom encompass us. Dying
is but going home." —Charles Spurgeon

"Live in Christ, live in Christ, and then the flesh need not
fear death." —John Knox

For more: Read the blog post "Going to the Party": epm.org/goingparty

Full of Grace and Truth

Truth hates sin. Grace loves sinners. Those full of grace and truth—those full of Jesus—do both.

H ate the sin, but love the sinner." Truth hates sin. Grace loves sinners. Those full of grace and truth—those full of Jesus—do both. "'Then neither do I condemn you,' Jesus declared. 'Go now and leave your life of sin'" (John 8:11, NIV).

Attempts to "soften" the gospel by minimizing truth keep people from Jesus. Attempts to "toughen" the gospel by minimizing grace keep people from Jesus. It's not enough for us to offer grace or truth. We must offer both.

When we offend everybody, we've declared truth without grace. When we offend nobody, we've watered down truth in the name of grace. John 1:14 tells us Jesus came "full of grace *and* truth." Let's not choose between them but be characterized by a balanced abundance of both.

Perspectives from God's Word

"The Word became flesh and dwelt among us, and we have seen his glory, glory as of the only Son from the Father, full of grace and truth" (John 1:14).

"The law was given through Moses; grace and truth came through Jesus Christ" (John 1:17).

Perspectives from God's People

"The ultimate test of our spirituality is the measure of our amazement at the grace of God." —D. Martyn Lloyd-Jones

"True happiness is to rejoice in the truth, for to rejoice in the truth is to rejoice in you, O God, who are the truth." —Augustine

For more: Watch the video "The Grace and Truth Paradox: Q&A": epm.org/gracetruth

Perspectives from God's Word

"According to his promise we are waiting for new heavens and a new earth in which righteousness dwells" (2 Peter 3:13).

"The creation itself will be set free from its bondage to corruption and obtain the freedom of the glory of the children of God" (Romans 8:21).

Perspectives from God's People

"We are earthlings. We were made to live here. This world is our home. For too long, many evangelical Christians have mistakenly believed that the goal of life is to escape the bounds of earth. . . . Heaven is merely the first leg of a journey that is round-trip." —Michael Wittmer

"Our destiny is an earthly one: a new earth, an earth redeemed and transfigured. An earth reunited with heaven, but an earth, nevertheless." —Paul Marshall

For more: Read the article "What Resurrection and the New Earth Will Mean": epm.org/resurrection

Awaiting Heaven on the (New) Earth

In the end Christ will finally and completely restore His entire creation to what God originally intended.

U topian idealists who dream of humanity creating "Heaven on Earth" are destined for disappointment. Their belief that humans can achieve perfection is mistaken. However, one day there *will* be Heaven on Earth. That's God's dream. It's God's plan. And He, not we, will accomplish it. "Now the dwelling of God is with men, and he will live with them" (Revelation 21:3, NIV).

If I promised you a new car, would you say, "If it's new, it probably won't have an engine, a transmission, doors, wheels, or windows"? No, you'd never make such assumptions. Why? Because if a new car didn't have these things, it wouldn't be a car. Likewise, when Scripture speaks of a New Earth (see 2 Peter 3:13; Revelation 21:1), we can expect that it will be a far better version of the old Earth, but it will truly be Earth.

Earth can be delivered only by being resurrected. The removal of the Curse will be as thorough and sweeping as the redemptive work of Christ. In bringing us salvation, Christ has already undone some of the damage in our hearts, but in the end He'll finally and completely restore His entire creation to what God originally intended.

Holiness and Happiness Together

*God made us to be happiest
when we pursue holiness. True
holiness and true happiness
are ultimately inseparable.*

D NA's double helix is perfectly balanced at the core of human life. Two strands wrap around each other, forming an axis of symmetry and providing a perfect complement for each other.

God designed holiness and happiness to enjoy a similar relationship: each is enhanced by the other. For those of us who are Christ-centered believers, our lives should overflow with both. Neither alone will suffice; both together are essential for the truly Christ-centered life.

When Jesus says, "Be perfect" (Matthew 5:48), we should recognize that true happiness in Him is part of what He intends. Our pleasure is won in the "Aha!" moments of discovering firsthand why God's ways really are best. As we grow in knowledge, we can increasingly join Paul in saying, "We have the mind of Christ" (1 Corinthians 2:16) on the things He has revealed. The more we discover God's ways and experience the goodness of His holiness, the less we try to find happiness apart from Him.

Perspectives from God's Word

"We know that our old self was crucified with him in order that the body of sin might be brought to nothing, so that we would no longer be enslaved to sin" (Romans 6:6).

"Glory in his holy name; let the hearts of those who seek the LORD rejoice!" (1 Chronicles 16:10).

Perspectives from God's People

"Every *wicked* man is a *miserable* man. God has wedded sin and misery as strongly as he has holiness and happiness. God hath joined them together; none can put them asunder." —Adam Clarke

"Sin is joy poisoned. Holiness is joy postponed and pursued." —Tony Reinke

For more: Read the blog post "Why We Don't Need to Choose Between Happiness and Holiness": epm.org/choose

A Theology
of Laughter

Who is the most intelligent, creative,
witty, and joyful human being
in the universe? Jesus Christ.

Often we think of ourselves as fun-loving and of God as a humorless killjoy. But we've got it backward. We are the boring ones, not God. Did we invent wit, humor, and laughter? No. God did. We'll never begin to exhaust God's sense of humor and His love for pleasure-filled joy. "You make known to me the path of life; in your presence there is fullness of joy; at your right hand are pleasures forevermore" (Psalm 16:11).

For Nanci and me, laughter is therapy. We love to laugh. As people instinctively blink to get something out of their eyes, we laugh to lighten our hearts. Have you ever laughed so hard it brought tears to your eyes? I think on the New Earth Christ will laugh with us, and His wit and fun-loving nature will be our greatest source of endless laughter. We need a biblical theology of humor that prepares us for an eternity of celebration and spontaneous laughter.

Who is the most intelligent, creative, witty, and joyful human being in the universe? Jesus Christ. Whose laughter will be loudest and most contagious on the New Earth? Jesus Christ's.

Perspectives from God's Word

"Then our mouth was filled with laughter, and our tongue with shouts of joy. . . . The LORD has done great things for us; we are glad" (Psalm 126:2-3).

"Happy are you who weep now, because you will laugh" (Luke 6:21, CEB).

Perspectives from God's People

"Our sense of humor is a gift from God which should be controlled as well as cultivated." —J. Oswald Sanders

"Let it not be imagined that the life of a good Christian must be a life of melancholy and gloominess; for he only resigns some pleasures to enjoy others infinitely better."
—Blaise Pascal

For more: Read the blog post "Laughter in Heaven": epm.org/laughterheaven

Defeating Lust, Feeding Right Passions

We become what we daily choose to take into our minds.

God made a universe in which righteousness is always rewarded and unrighteousness is always punished, though not always immediately. Purity is always smart; impurity is always stupid. If we plant purity today, we will reap a rich harvest.

The problem isn't passion but lust. We serve a passionate God. We should love and serve Him passionately. But we need to cultivate a passion for the right objects. "Each of you should learn to control his own body" (1 Thessalonians 4:4, NIV) means self-control doesn't come naturally; it requires training and discipline.

Lust is fed by whatever we've deposited in our brains that it can get its claws on. The kind of person we are becoming is determined by what we choose daily to take into our minds. When we read Scripture and good books, participate in godly discussions, and care for the needy, we are inclining ourselves toward righteousness. "For out of the heart come evil thoughts, murder, adultery, sexual immorality" (Matthew 15:19).

Perspectives from God's Word

"I the LORD search the heart and test the mind, to give every man according to his ways, according to the fruit of his deeds" (Jeremiah 17:10).

"If you live according to the flesh you will die, but if by the Spirit you put to death the deeds of the body, you will live" (Romans 8:13).

Perspectives from God's People

"Saving grace makes a Christian as willing to leave his sin as a slave is willing to leave his galley, or a prisoner his dungeon, or a thief his bolts, or a beggar his rags." —Thomas Brooks

"Imagination is a God-given gift; but if it is fed dirt by the eye, it will be dirty. All sin, not least sexual sin, begins with the imagination. Therefore, what feeds the imagination is of maximum importance in the pursuit of kingdom righteousness." —D. A. Carson

For more: Read the article "Protecting Purity in a Technological Corinth": epm.org/protectpurity

Delighting in Him

*Time with God is the fountain
from which holiness, joy, and
delight flow. It reminds us who
we are and whose we are.*

Have you been sitting at the feet of Jesus, as Mary of Bethany did (see Luke 10:38–42)? Have you been turning your back on a thousand distractions to enjoy the presence of your Bridegroom, the Carpenter from Nazareth, the One who said He was going to prepare a place for you and is coming back to get you so you can be with Him forever (see John 14:2–3)?

Time with God is the fountain from which holiness flows, along with joy and delight. It reminds us who we are and whose we are. Paul tells us, "Our citizenship is in heaven" (Philippians 3:20). We are "aliens and strangers on earth," who are "longing for a better country—a heavenly one" (Hebrews 11:13, 16, NIV).

If we delight ourselves in God, that will transform the desires of our hearts. We will want what He wants. We will want His closeness, and the desire of our hearts will be to hear Him say to us, "Well done." And when that day comes, He will flood us with more joy that we can imagine. He will say, "Enter into the joy of your master" (Matthew 25:21, 23).

Perspectives from God's Word

"I long for your salvation, O LORD, and your law is my delight" (Psalm 119:174).

"Delight yourself in the LORD, and he will give you the desires of your heart" (Psalm 37:4).

Perspectives from God's People

"God's greatest interest is to glorify the wealth of his grace by making sinners happy in him." —John Piper

"God cannot give us a happiness and peace apart from Himself, because it is not there. There is no such thing." —C. S. Lewis

For more: Read the article "Can't You See That I'm Busy?": epm.org/busy

He Suffered the Most

Isn't it astonishing that God would willingly, premeditatedly create a world in which no one would suffer more than He?

I n this world of suffering and evil, I have a profound and abiding hope, and faith for the future—not because I follow a set of religious rules to make me better, but because for over forty years I've known a real Person, and today I know Him better than ever. Through inconceivable self-sacrifice, He has touched me deeply, given me a new heart, and utterly transformed my life.

Some people can't believe God would create a world in which people would suffer so much. Isn't it astonishing that God would create a world in which no one would suffer more than He? His physical suffering was horrible, but His anguish in taking our sin on Himself was far worse (see 2 Corinthians 5:21). That God willingly, with ancient premeditation, intentionally endured the cross for us is utterly stunning.

Whenever you feel tempted to ask God "Why did you do this to me?" look at the cross and ask, "Why did you do that *for* me?"

Perspectives from God's Word

"I lay down my life for the sheep. . . . No one takes it from me, but I lay it down of my own accord" (John 10:15, 18).

"I will divide him a portion with the many, and he shall divide the spoil with the strong, because he poured out his soul to death and was numbered with the transgressors; yet he bore the sin of many, and makes intercession for the transgressors" (Isaiah 53:12).

Perspectives from God's People

"When anything disagreeable and displeasing happens to you, remember Christ crucified and be silent." —Saint John of the Cross

"Cast your arms around the cross of Christ, and give up your heart to God, and then, come what may, I am persuaded that 'Neither death, nor life, nor angels, nor principalities, nor powers, nor things present, nor things to come, nor height, nor depth, nor any other creature, shall be able to separate us from the love of God, which is in Christ Jesus our Lord.'" —Charles Spurgeon

For more: Read the blog post "The Sentence Against God": epm.org/sentence

Let's Be Grateful

If only we could see our situation clearly. Anything less than gratitude? Unthinkable! He owes us nothing. We owe Him everything.

The Word of God is a corrective to the spirit of entitlement and ingratitude that's poisoning our culture, and too often the church as well. We are never grateful for what we think we deserve. On the contrary, we gripe and complain and think God and others are unfair if it doesn't come to us.

If only we could see our situation clearly—even for a moment. We deserve expulsion; He gives us a diploma. We deserve the electric chair; He gives us a parade. Anything less than overwhelming gratitude should be unthinkable. He owes us nothing. We owe Him everything.

Perhaps a parent's greatest heritage to pass on to a child is the ability to perceive the multitude of God's daily blessings and to respond with continual gratitude, "abounding in thanksgiving" (Colossians 2:7).

Perspectives from God's Word

"[Give] thanks to the Father, who has qualified you to share in the inheritance of the saints in light. He has delivered us" (Colossians 1:12–13).

"Give thanks in all circumstances" (1 Thessalonians 5:18).

Perspectives from God's People

"Gratitude is not just for private consumption but for public conversation." —Nancy DeMoss Wolgemuth

"I would maintain that thanks are the highest form of thought; and that gratitude is happiness doubled by wonder." —G. K. Chesterton

For more: Read the blog post "Gratitude: God's Will for Us": epm.org/gratitude

To Be Known by God Is Enough

God will evaluate our service for Him now on Earth to determine how we'll serve Him on the New Earth.

We say we want to be God's servants and to serve others. Yet there are few things we resent more than being treated like servants. May God give us the heart of a faithful servant who is first about God, second about others, and third about ourselves.

Scripture teaches that God will evaluate our service for Him on the present Earth to determine how we'll serve Him on the New Earth. The humble servant will be put in charge of much, whereas the one who has lorded it over others in the present world will have power taken away: "Everyone who exalts himself will be humbled, and he who humbles himself will be exalted" (Luke 14:11).

Being well known here doesn't matter. Hearing God say "Well done" does. To be known by God: it doesn't get any better than that!

Perspectives from God's Word

"Even the Son of Man did not come to be served but to serve, and to give his life as a ransom for many" (Mark 10:45, NET).

"His master said to him, 'Well done, good and faithful servant. You have been faithful over a little; I will set you over much. Enter into the joy of your master'" (Matthew 25:21).

Perspectives from God's People

"Christ's followers cannot expect better treatment in the world than their Master had. . . . Let them not promise themselves more honor or pleasure in the world than Christ had. . . . Let him live a life of labour and self-denial as his Master doth, and make himself a servant of all; let him stoop, and let him toil, and do all the good he can, and then he will be a complete disciple." —Matthew Henry

"Where Jesus does not shine, the soul is sick. Bask in His beams, and you shall be vigorous in the service of your Lord." —Charles Spurgeon

For more: Read the blog post "What Does a Cross Bearer Look Like?": epm.org/crossbearer

Prayer: Making an Eternal Difference

We pray, believing our prayers are making an eternal difference; we anticipate Heaven, where we'll learn God's breathtaking answers.

God's greatest works, accomplished through prayer, are often invisible to us now. We pray now in faith, believing our prayers are making an eternal difference; we anticipate Heaven, where we'll learn God's breathtaking answers to our prayers, including many that seemed to go unheard and were ignored.

Prayer isn't passive; it's active. It's really doing something. Prayer isn't the least we can do; it's the most. "Pray in the Spirit on all occasions with all kinds of prayers and requests" (Ephesians 6:18, NIV).

James 1:5 says we don't have wisdom because we don't ask for it, so prayer is critical in seeking and living the will of God. When we are controlled by the Spirit, we won't commit the acts of the sinful nature (see Galatians 5:19–21) but will produce the fruit of the Spirit (see verses 22–23). When we're in God's will, we'll participate in worshipping the Lord, teaching one another, giving thanks to God, and serving others (see Ephesians 5:17–33).

Perspectives from God's Word

"Pray without ceasing" (1 Thessalonians 5:17).

"[Gabriel told Daniel,] 'At the beginning of your pleas for mercy a word went out'" (Daniel 9:23).

Perspectives from God's People

"We don't believe 'in the power of prayer,' but in our all-powerful God who empowers our inherently powerless prayers." —Burk Parsons

"The Christian on his knees sees more than the philosopher on tiptoe." —D. L. Moody

For more: Read the article "Perspectives on Prayer from Daniel 9–10": epm.org/prayerperspectives

"Let us not grow weary of doing good, for in due season we will reap, if we do not give up" (Galatians 6:9).

Perspectives from God's People

"The Christian is a person who makes it easy for others to believe in God." —Robert Murray M'Cheyne

"We know too little of true Christianity if we do not feel a deep concern about the souls of unconverted people." —J. C. Ryle

For more: Read the blog post "Truth, Grace, and My Father's Conversion at Age 84": epm.org/fathersconversion

Offering Jesus to Those Who Thirst

In the parched wastelands of this Earth, God calls us to offer refreshment—Jesus— to the multitudes dying of thirst.

The world already has itself. It yearns not for what it has but for what can come only from outside: the good news of Jesus. We proclaim "our Savior Christ Jesus, who abolished death and brought life and immortality to light through the gospel" (2 Timothy 1:10).

As long as we're still here in the parched wastelands of the present Earth, God calls us to offer refreshment to the multitudes dying of thirst. What should we offer them? Exactly what they thirst for: a Person and a place. Jesus is that Person. Heaven is that place.

Have you been praying for years for someone's salvation without any visible results? Don't get discouraged. Just keep on praying, witnessing, giving the person helpful books, giving of your time and affection. Be faithful to your Lord and leave the results to Him.

Perspectives from God's Word

"Go therefore and make disciples of all nations" (Matthew 28:19).

The Audience of One

Jesus is the Audience of One. Let's live for the applause of God, not for the praise of men.

We should do what we believe pleases our Lord, regardless of how it ranks in opinion polls. That includes loving others and giving radically, ministering to the down and out, addressing addictions, and saying we think it's wrong to kill humans of all ages, including the unborn. We do such things not seeking the approval of our culture but of our King, entrusting ourselves "to him who judges justly" (1 Peter 2:23).

Paul said, "If I were still trying to please man, I would not be a servant of Christ" (Galatians 1:10). Jesus is the Audience of One. We will stand before His judgment seat, no one else's. We should long to hear Him say, "Well done, good and faithful servant." If we live for the approval of others and not for Christ's approval, our commitment will not last.

John Chrysostom, an early church father, said, "Men who are in love with applause have their spirits starved not only when they are blamed off-hand, but even when they fail to be constantly praised."[6] It was said of some religious leaders that "they loved praise from men more than praise from God" (John 12:43, NIV). Let's live our lives not for the praise of men, but for the applause of God, the Audience of One.

Perspectives from God's Word

"Whether we are at home or away, we make it our aim to please him" (2 Corinthians 5:9).

"Whatever you do, work heartily, as for the Lord and not for men, knowing that from the Lord you will receive the inheritance as your reward. You are serving the Lord Christ" (Colossians 3:23–24).

Perspectives from God's People

"Now think, my brother, you will be in heaven very soon. Since last year a great number have gone home: before next year many more will have ascended to glory. Sitting up in those celestial seats, how shall we wish that we had lived below?" —Charles Spurgeon

"The beginning of true nobility comes when a man ceases to be interested in the judgment of men and becomes interested in the judgment of God." —J. Gresham Machen

For more: Read the article "Living a Life of Grace and Truth for the Audience of One": epm.org/audienceofone

God's Glory, Our Good

We think God calls us to do things that won't be good for us. In fact, that which is for God's glory is for our good.

S atan has conned many people into a twisted view of the Christian life. We imagine that God calls us to do things that won't be good for us, while the unbelievers are out there having all the fun. In fact, anything done for God's glory also works for our good.

Choosing what is good and right will always be to our advantage. Wrongdoing sometimes appears to offer benefits, and doing right may seem to bring serious disadvantages. But in the long run, in this life and in the afterlife, God rewards His children's right choices and confers consequences (not eternal punishment) for wrong ones. "A man reaps what he sows" (Galatians 6:7, NIV).

What is in God's best interests is also in others' best interests and in my best interests, not necessarily immediately but always in the end. Something that is good will be good for everyone, not good for God and bad for me, or good for me and bad for my neighbor. Each time I obey God, I'm doing what's ultimately best for all.

Perspectives from God's Word

"Who is the man who fears the LORD? Him will he instruct in the way that he should choose. His soul shall abide in well-being, and his offspring shall inherit the land" (Psalm 25:12–13).

"The simple are killed by their turning away, and the complacency of fools destroys them; but whoever listens to me will dwell secure and will be at ease, without dread of disaster" (Proverbs 1:32–33).

Perspectives from God's People

"God has not created a universe where you must choose between your joy and his glory." —John Piper

"Since man was made for the glory of God, he can never be what he was intended to be until his life is properly focused on the glory of God. . . . So God's glory does not detract from man's life. Instead, His glory is the sun around which the whole of life must revolve if there is to be the light and life of God in our experience." —Sinclair Ferguson

For more: Read the article "The Cost of Discipleship": epm.org/costdiscipleship

The Hell We Deserve

Heaven is not our default destination.
No one goes there automatically.

For every American who believes he's going to Hell, there are 120 who believe they're going to Heaven.[7] This optimism stands in stark contrast to Jesus Christ's words written in the Bible: "For the gate is narrow and the way is hard that leads to life, and those who find it are few" (Matthew 7:14).

The truth is, according to the Bible, we don't automatically go to Heaven. In fact, Hell—not Heaven—is our default destination. Unless our sin problem is solved once and for all, we can't enter Heaven. That's the bad news.

But once that's straight in our minds, we're ready to hear the good news of Jesus Christ: Jesus took upon Himself, on the cross, the Hell we deserve so that we could experience for eternity the Heaven we don't deserve!

If we imagine we deserve Heaven, not Hell, then the "good news" isn't deliverance from something horrible and therefore isn't such good news after all. A person who lives in safety and luxury today doesn't consider it radically good news that he'll live in safety and luxury tomorrow. The gospel speaks loudest to those who recognize their spiritual poverty, not to those who think they are fine just as they are.

Perspectives from God's Word

"Strive to enter through the narrow door. For many, I tell you, will seek to enter and will not be able" (Luke 13:24).

"Whoever has my commandments and keeps them, he it is who loves me. And he who loves me will be loved by my Father, and I will love him and manifest myself to him" (John 14:21).

Perspectives from God's People

"When the heart no longer feels the truth of hell, the gospel passes from *good* news to just news. The intensity of joy is blunted and the heart-spring of love is dried up."
—John Piper

"Christ is not one of many ways to approach God, nor is He the best of several ways; He is the only way."
—A. W. Tozer

For more: Read the article "Can You Know You're Going to Heaven?": epm.org/knowheaven

Giving Our Burdens to Him

Many hear God say, "Do more," not "I've done it for you—rest." Yet Jesus said, "My yoke is easy, and my burden is light."

Sometimes, in moments of pride, we need to fear God and repent. Other times, in moments of brokenness and despair, we need to just bathe in His grace and see His smile and hear Him say, "Well done. . . . Enter into the joy of your master" (Matthew 25:21, 23). We're told to cast our "cares on him because he cares for" us (1 Peter 5:7, NET), and come to Him . . . and He will give us His peace (see John 14:27).

I learned years ago that I have to say no to the great majority of things I'm asked to do, so I'm available to say yes to those few God wants me to do. Jesus calls upon us to carry our crosses yet paradoxically promises a light burden and rest for our souls. If the burden feels heavy and our souls aren't at rest, maybe we've picked up more than He intended us to carry or we haven't fully come to Him.

Many think they hear God say, "Do more" and "Do better." But not, "I've done it for you—rest." Yet this is what Jesus meant when He said, "Come to me, all who labor and are heavy laden. . . . Take my yoke upon you, and learn from me. . . . For my yoke is easy, and my burden is light" (Matthew 11:28–30).

Perspectives from God's Word

"Cast your burden on the LORD, and he will sustain you; he will never permit the righteous to be moved" (Psalm 55:22).

"For God alone my soul waits in silence; from him comes my salvation" (Psalm 62:1).

Perspectives from God's People

"I'm convinced that one of the major reasons we can't handle the demands of day-to-day living is that our *spirits* are weary. Our *souls* need to be restored. . . . The restoration of our souls is a ministry of our Great Shepherd. . . . If I don't take time to get my spiritual tank refilled, I soon find myself 'running on fumes.'" —Nancy DeMoss Wolgemuth

"The eternal rest of the Gospel is this—God's affection for you isn't rooted in your performance, but in Christ's." —Paul Tripp

For more: Read the blog post "Enjoying Rest, Now and in the Life to Come": epm.org/enjoyingrest

Good Works and God's Glory

Our Lord applauds righteous
works done for the right reasons,
for His glory and not ours.

In Revelation 19:7–8 we're told, " 'The wedding of the Lamb has come, and his bride has made herself ready. Fine linen, bright and clean, was given her to wear.' (Fine linen stands for the righteous acts of the saints.)" (NIV). Note the parenthetical statement in the verse. I once cited this verse in a book, and the editor "corrected" it, assuming it was my interpretation. It didn't sound right. But it is; it's Scripture!

Somewhere we've gotten the erroneous idea that, to God, *works* is a dirty word. This is totally false. While He condemns works done to earn salvation and works done to impress others, our Lord enthusiastically *commends* righteous works done for the right reasons: for His glory, not for ours.

God created us to do good works, has a lifetime of good works for each of us to do, and will reward us according to whether or not we do them. Indeed, Scripture ties God's reward-giving to His very character: "God is not unjust; he will not forget your work and the love you have shown him as you have helped his people and continue to help them" (Hebrews 6:10, NIV).

Perspectives from God's Word

"Let your light shine before others, so that they may see your good works and give glory to your Father who is in heaven" (Matthew 5:16).

"By grace you have been saved through faith. And this is not your own doing; it is the gift of God, not a result of works, so that no one may boast. For we are his workmanship, created in Christ Jesus for good works, which God prepared beforehand, that we should walk in them" (Ephesians 2:8–10).

Perspectives from God's People

"Truly, if faith is there, [the believer] cannot hold back; he . . . breaks out into good works." —Martin Luther

"If we had choice of a sphere in which we could serve God with widest range, we should choose not heaven but earth. There are no slums and over-crowded rooms in heaven to which we can go with help, but there are plenty of them here." —Charles Spurgeon

For more: Read the article "What Is a Godly Perspective on Doing Good Works?": epm.org/goodworks

Thinking like Stewards, Not Owners

If God owns it all, shouldn't we regularly ask Him, "What do You want me to do with Your money and possessions?"

When it comes to money and possessions, whenever we think like owners, it's a red flag. We should be thinking like stewards or investment managers, always looking for the best place to invest the Owner's money. At the end of our term of service, we'll undergo a job performance evaluation: "Each of us will give an account of himself to God" (Romans 14:12).

If we really believe God is the owner of all that has been entrusted to us, shouldn't we regularly ask Him, "What do You want me to do with Your money and Your possessions?" And shouldn't we be open to the possibility that He may want us to share large portions of His assets with those in need?

Jesus made a powerful correlation between our present handling of earthly wealth and His future decision to entrust to our care another kind of wealth. "If you are untrustworthy about worldly wealth, who will trust you with the true riches of heaven?" (Luke 16:11, NLT). There is a direct connection between our faithful use of money here and now, and the "true riches" we will oversee in His future Kingdom.

Perspectives from God's Word

"As for the rich in this present age, . . . they are to do good, to be rich in good works, to be generous and ready to share" (1 Timothy 6:17–18).

"We are more happy when we give than when we receive" (Acts 20:35, NLV).

Perspectives from God's People

"Find out how much God has given you and from it take what you need; the remainder is needed by others."
—Augustine

"Let us walk as *stewards* and not act as owners, keeping for ourselves the means with which the Lord has entrusted us. He has not blessed us that we may gratify our own carnal mind but for the sake of using our money in His service and to His praise." —George Müller

For more: Watch the video "FedEx Guy: Are We Being God's Delivery People?": epm.org/deliverypeople

When It Comes to Heaven, Dream Big

As we get older, reality sinks in and our childhood dreams shrink. But when the Curse is reversed, our greatest dreams will be revived and lived out.

Those who know God and believe His promise of bodily resurrection can dream great dreams: Skydiving without a parachute? Maybe. Scuba diving without an air tank? Will we be able to tolerate diving hundreds of feet without special equipment? I hope so. We know that our resurrection bodies will be superior. Won't it be fantastic to test their limits, with no possibility of injury or death? One day we will live our dreams, with Jesus.

When we're young, we dream of becoming astronauts or athletes. As we get older, our dreams shrink and realism sinks in. When the Curse is reversed, our dreams will be revived, enhanced, and lived out. Perhaps that's part of why childlikeness is necessary for Heaven. "Let the little children come to me, . . . for the kingdom of heaven belongs to such as these" (Matthew 19:14, NIV).

"No longer will there be any curse" (Revelation 22:3, NIV). The hope, the promise, the anticipation of this verse is inexpressible—it is weighty, thick with promise and joy. Let your imagination go where this verse leads you. Write it down, and post it on your refrigerator and dashboard and bathroom mirror.

Perspectives from God's Word

"Beloved, we are God's children now, and what we will be has not yet appeared; but we know that when he appears we shall be like him, because we shall see him as he is" (1 John 3:2).

"Our citizenship is in heaven, and from it we await a Savior, the Lord Jesus Christ, who will transform our lowly body to be like his glorious body, by the power that enables him even to subject all things to himself" (Philippians 3:20–21).

Perspectives from God's People

"However miserable, powerless and contemptible in life and death [our bodies are], Christ will at his coming render our bodies beautiful, pure, shining and worthy of honor, until they correspond to his own immortal, glorious body."
—Martin Luther

"The best is yet to be." —John Wesley

For more: Watch the video "What Will Our Resurrected Bodies Be Like?": epm.org/resurrectedbodies

The Right Perspective in Suffering

If we have an eternal future as resurrected people living under King Jesus, no present suffering will prove worthless.

N o matter how strong the body and how positive the circumstances, a crushed spirit will never experience joy. Perspective is what makes the spirit soar like an eagle even when the body is ravaged by accident, disease, and age. A right attitude carries you through bad circumstances and poor health.

If we have no eternal future as resurrected people living under the benevolent rule of King Jesus, then our present sufferings will ultimately have no value. If we have such a future, however, then no present suffering—regardless of its scope—will prove worthless. In fact, such sufferings are a means to an end: incalculable future goodness.

Shouldn't we suppose that many of our most painful ordeals will look quite different a million years from now as we recall them on the New Earth? What if one day we discover that God has wasted nothing in our lives on Earth? What if we see that every agony was part of giving birth to eternal joy?

Perspectives from God's Word

"This light momentary affliction is preparing for us an eternal weight of glory beyond all comparison" (2 Corinthians 4:17).

"I consider that the sufferings of this present time are not worth comparing with the glory that is to be revealed to us" (Romans 8:18).

Perspectives from God's People

"I want to stay in the habit of 'glancing' at my problems and 'gazing' at the Lord." —Joni Eareckson Tada

"There are rare and wonderful species of joy that flourish only in the rainy atmosphere of suffering." —John Piper

For more: Watch the video "The God Who Will Bring Good out of Bad (Romans 8:28)": epm.org/bringgood

A Passion to Know the King of Kings

*Don't let life just happen to you—choose
to invest your days in what matters.*

We tend to be passionate about things that don't matter, fanatics and fans about what won't last. But we are afraid to look like fanatics for Jesus. We seem determined to dole Jesus out in acceptable portions, unwilling to appear fools for Christ. What a loss! Consider the example of John Wesley, who was asked about the key to his ministry. He supposedly said, "I ask God to set me on fire and let people watch me burn."

I thank God that today I don't just love Jesus as much as I used to; I love Him more. That is to His credit, and I'm deeply grateful. He's what makes it so exciting and so worthwhile, and He's the One who empowers me to walk what's been called "a long obedience in the same direction." More than ever, I want to know Christ. How about you?

Give Jesus first place in your life. Don't just let your life happen to you; choose what to do with it, or in the end you'll wonder where it went. If you're going to persevere as Christ's follower, you must consciously choose not to squander your life or let it idle away, but to invest it in what matters.

Perspectives from God's Word

"I want to know Christ and the power of his resurrection and the fellowship of sharing in his sufferings" (Philippians 3:10, NIV).

"Look carefully then how you walk, not as unwise but as wise, making the best use of the time" (Ephesians 5:15–16).

Perspectives from God's People

"The Fort Knox of faith is Christ. Fellowshipping with him. Walking with him. Pondering him. Exploring him. The heart-stopping realization that in him you are part of something ancient, endless, unstoppable, and unfathomable." —Max Lucado

"The longer you know Christ, and the nearer you come to him, still the more do you see of his glory. Every farther prospect of Christ entertains the mind with a fresh delight. He is as it were a new Christ every day, and yet the same Christ still." —John Flavel

For more: Read the blog post "How Can I Stay Motivated in My Relationship with Jesus Christ?": epm.org/motivated

The One in Charge

The God of providence weaves together millions of details into our lives. His thoughts and ways are far above ours.

We are not the cosmic center: God is. He holds the universe, and each of us, in His gravity. When we make ourselves the center of gravity, we attempt to hold God in orbit around us. Then we draw false conclusions. For example, whenever we don't get our way, we assume it must mean God isn't really there.

God is the Source of all good and the standard by which good is measured. We may not like what God does, but we're in no position to accuse Him of wrongdoing. Every breath He gives us is a gift. But if you want to hear Him say He cares about you and sympathizes with you, listen to what He says to His people: "As a father shows compassion to his children, so the LORD shows compassion to those who fear him" (Psalm 103:13).

The God of providence weaves millions of details into our lives and the lives around us. Maybe He doesn't have one big reason for bringing a certain person, success, failure, disease, or accident into our lives; God may have hundreds of little reasons. In order to understand His explanations, we'd have to be God. " 'For my thoughts are not your thoughts, neither are your ways my ways,' declares the LORD" (Isaiah 55:8, NIV).

Perspectives from God's Word

"You are great and do wondrous things; you alone are God" (Psalm 86:10).

"The LORD answered Job out of the whirlwind and said: . . . 'Who has first given to me, that I should repay him? Whatever is under the whole heaven is mine'" (Job 40:6; 41:11).

Perspectives from God's People

"What comes into our minds when we think about God is the most important thing about us." —A. W. Tozer

"He who demands a reason of God is not in a fit state to receive one." —Charles Spurgeon

For more: Read the blog post "There Is No Pointless Suffering": epm.org/pointless

The Awesomeness of God's Creation

Creatively speaking, God is just "warming up" in our universe.

On Mars, the volcano Olympus Mons rises more than eighty-four thousand feet, nearly three times higher than Mount Everest, with a base that would cover the state of Arizona. The Valles Marineris is a vast canyon that stretches one-seventh of the way around Mars. Dozens of our Grand Canyons could fit inside it.

The New Earth may have far more spectacular planetary features than these, and the New Heavens may have greater stars, nebulae, and galaxies than our current cosmos. On the present Earth, God shows Himself through natural wonders. Since the old Earth is the prototype of the new, there's every reason to believe He will show His greatness and beauty the same way on the New Earth.

Imagine what we might find on the new Mars or the new Saturn and Jupiter and their magnificent moons. I remember vividly the thrill of first seeing Saturn's rings through my new telescope when I was ten years old. Five years later, I heard the gospel for the first time and came to know Jesus, but the wonders of the heavens helped lead me to God. How many times in the new universe will we be stunned by the awesomeness of God's creation?

Perspectives from God's Word

"My own hands stretched out the heavens; I marshaled their starry hosts" (Isaiah 45:12, NIV).

"My own hand laid the foundations of the earth, and my right hand spread out the heavens; when I summon them, they all stand up together" (Isaiah 48:13, NIV).

Perspectives from God's People

"The physical world exists pre-eminently to display for our eternal joy the artistic creativity, endless power, and manifold wisdom of its Creator, the Son, our Lord Jesus Christ." —Sam Storms

"Beauty is both a gift and a map. It is a gift to be enjoyed and a map to be followed back to the source of the beauty with praise and thanksgiving." —Steve DeWitt

For more: Read the article "What Does the Bible Mean by the Term 'New Heavens'?": epm.org/meaningheavens

Yielding to the Sculptor's Chisel

Like a master sculptor making a marble block into something magnificent, God has called us to yield ourselves to His chisel.

To produce one of his masterpieces, the statue *David,* Michelangelo chose a stone all other artists had rejected. Seeing that marble block's hidden potential, he chipped away everything that wasn't David. Now, if marble had feelings, it might have resented its sculptor. While Michelangelo may not have called upon the stone to cooperate with him, God has called us to yield ourselves by submitting to His chisel.

Jesus said in Matthew 13:43, "Then the righteous will shine like the sun in the kingdom of their Father." This transformation does not simply happen after we die. It starts here and now in this world. And suffering is the instrument that makes us shine (see 1 Peter 1:6–7). God isn't just preparing a place for us. He is preparing us for that place.

If God brought eternal joy through the suffering of Jesus, can He bring eternal joy through my present suffering and yours? If Jesus endured His suffering through anticipating the reward of unending joy, can He empower us to do the same?

Perspectives from God's Word

"[Jesus], who for the joy that was set before him endured the cross, despising the shame, and is seated at the right hand of the throne of God" (Hebrews 12:2).

"Sing for joy, O heavens! Rejoice, O earth! Burst into song, O mountains! For the LORD has comforted his people and will have compassion on them in their suffering" (Isaiah 49:13, NLT).

Perspectives from God's People

"Being satisfied in God (or anything) always seems easier when all is going well. But when things you love are being stripped out of your hands, then the test is real. If God remains precious in those moments, then his supreme worth shines more brightly. He is most glorified." —John Piper

"That is what mortals misunderstand. They say of some temporal suffering, 'No future bliss can make up for it,' not knowing that Heaven, once attained, will work backwards and turn even that agony into a glory." —C. S. Lewis

For more: Read the blog post "Affliction Was Necessary to Me": epm.org/affliction

Feasting and Fellowship

*One day we'll feast together on the New
Earth with the saints who have gone before,
celebrating the greatness of King Jesus.*

In Heaven, will we spend time with people whose lives are recorded in Scripture and church history? No doubt. Jesus told us we'll sit at the dinner table with Abraham, Isaac, and Jacob (see Matthew 8:11). If we sit with them, we should expect to sit with others. What do people do at dinner tables? In Middle Eastern cultures, dinner was, and is, not only about good food and drink but also a time for building relationships, talking together, and telling stories.

Whom do you look forward to meeting when you get to Heaven? I look forward to reconnecting with many old friends as well as my mom and dad. I look forward to thanking C. S. Lewis, Francis Schaeffer, and A. W. Tozer for how their writings have changed me. I anticipate meeting William Carey, Hudson Taylor, Amy Carmichael, Jim Elliot, Charles Spurgeon, D. L. Moody, Harriet Beecher Stowe, some of the *Amistad* slaves, William Wilberforce, and a host of others.

I thank the Lord for the countless believers—from times and places way beyond my reach—whom God has sovereignly used to draw me to Him. I long for the day when I'll sit by them at feasts on the New Earth, where we'll look at King Jesus and celebrate His greatness and works.

Perspectives from God's Word

"On this mountain the LORD of hosts will make for all peoples a feast of rich food, a feast of well-aged wine" (Isaiah 25:6).

"I tell you, many will come from east and west and recline at table with Abraham, Isaac, and Jacob in the kingdom of heaven" (Matthew 8:11).

Perspectives from God's People

"I know that Christ is all in all, and that it is the presence of God that makes heaven to be heaven. But yet it much sweetens the thoughts of that place to me, to remember that there is such a multitude of my most dear and precious friends in Christ." —Richard Baxter

"You'll be able to go down to the corner of Gold Street and Silver Boulevard, run into Abraham, and ask him a few questions. . . . You can ask Jonah what it felt like to be swallowed by a fish and live inside of it for three days." —Tony Evans

For more: Read the blog post "Creator and Culture, and Anticipating a Redeemed Earth": epm.org/redeemedearth

A Heart for the Poor and Needy

The good Samaritan wasn't responsible for the plight of the wounded man, but he was responsible to love him as his neighbor.

Caring for the poor is a sobering responsibility for which we will all be held accountable. Helping the poor and homeless is not a peripheral issue. God links our efforts for the poor directly to our relationship with Him. May He one day say of us what He said of King Josiah: "He judged the cause of the poor and needy; then it was well. Is not this to know me? declares the LORD" (Jeremiah 22:16).

The good Samaritan was not responsible for the plight of the man lying beside the road. After all, he had not robbed and brutalized him. Nonetheless, he was responsible to love his neighbor as himself. He did this not simply by refraining from hurting him but by actively helping him. He generously used his time, energy, and money to care for him. Jesus instructed us to do the same (see Luke 10:30–37).

Our instinct is to give to those who will give us something in return. But Jesus told us to give to "the poor, the crippled, the lame, the blind. . . . Although they cannot repay you, you will be repaid at the resurrection of the righteous" (Luke 14:13–14, NIV). If we give to those who can't reward us, Christ guarantees He will personally reward us in Heaven.

Perspectives from God's Word

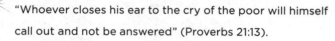

"Whoever closes his ear to the cry of the poor will himself call out and not be answered" (Proverbs 21:13).

"The King will answer them, 'Truly, I say to you, as you did it to one of the least of these my brothers, you did it to me'" (Matthew 25:40).

Perspectives from God's People

"The less I spent on myself and the more I gave to others the fuller of happiness and blessing did my soul become."
—Hudson Taylor

"Do all the good you can, by all the means you can, in all the ways you can, in all the places you can, at all the times you can, to all the people you can, as ever you can."
—John Wesley

For more: Read the blog post "Caring for the Needy: What God Says": epm.org/caringneedy

Imperfect Church, but Chosen Bride

Jesus calls the church His bride. Those who walk away from church walk away from Christ's redemptive work.

Jesus calls the church His bride. He died for her, and He says that ultimately the gates of Hell won't prevail against her. If you walk away from church, you walk away from Christ's redemptive work.

I understand all the hurts people have experienced in churches. Nanci and I have endured them also. A few times I have very much wanted to walk away and just go it on my own, seeking private fellowship with believers here and there. I haven't done so because I don't see the biblical liberty. (And after sticking with the church, in retrospect I'm very glad I didn't leave.) The church of the New Testament is not just the universal invisible body of Christ but actual local gatherings of imperfect people, with imperfect leaders, including elders who teach and lead, where there is actual accountability, and yes, when necessary, even discipline.

Many Christ-loving church families are scattered around the world. None are perfect, but many seek to honor Christ. Despite past bad experiences, I encourage people to not give up on local churches but to find one and invest themselves in helping it become more Christ-centered.*

---

* Our ministry has helped hundreds of people find Bible-believing churches near them. Contact us at epm.org/connect if you want help.

Perspectives from God's Word

"Christ loved the church and gave himself up for her" (Ephesians 5:25).

"Let us not neglect our meeting together, as some people do, but encourage one another, especially now that the day of his return is drawing near" (Hebrews 10:25, NLT).

Perspectives from God's People

"Being disconnected from the local church, for whatever reason, is a dangerous way to live . . . like lone sheep away from the safety of the flock and the watchful care of the shepherd, [these lone rangers] are vulnerable to predators of every sort." —Nancy DeMoss Wolgemuth

"To gather with God's people in united adoration of the Father is as necessary to the Christian life as prayer." —Martin Luther

For more: Read the blog post "Uncoolness, Tolerance, and Christ's Bride the Church": epm.org/uncoolness

The Sure Hope of Resurrection

Our society's white-knuckled grip on youthfulness is, ultimately, futile. But the gospel promises us eternal youthfulness in God's presence.

In our society many people look to cosmetic surgeries, implants, and other methods to remodel their crumbling bodies. We hold to youthfulness with a white-knuckled grip. Ultimately it's all in vain. But the gospel promises us eternal health, beauty, and happiness in the presence of our God and our spiritual family. It's not ours now—but it will be, in the resurrection.

In reference to the coming resurrection, Paul wrote, "But hope that is seen is no hope at all. Who hopes for what he already has? But if we hope for what we do not yet have, we wait for it patiently" (Romans 8:24–25, NIV). To many of us, "hope" sounds wishful and tentative, but *biblical hope* means "to anticipate with trust." We expect a sure thing, purchased on the Cross, accomplished and promised by an all-knowing God.

David wrote, "Thank you for making me so wonderfully complex! Your workmanship is marvelous" (Psalm 139:14, NLT). If our fallen bodies are so remarkable, how much more amazing will our resurrection bodies be? Will our eyes be able to function alternately as telescopes and microscopes? Will we be able to see new colors? Will our sense of smell be far more acute in a world where all smells will be good? Perhaps. I can't wait to find out!

Perspectives from God's Word

"O death, where is your victory?" (1 Corinthians 15:55).

"Jesus said to her, 'I am the resurrection and the life. Whoever believes in me, though he die, yet shall he live'" (John 11:25).

Perspectives from God's People

"Peter was made to walk on water in his old body. Imagine what Christ will enable you to do in your new one?" —Larry Dick

"No other religion, no other philosophy promises new bodies, hearts, and minds. Only in the Gospel of Christ do hurting people find such incredible hope." —Joni Eareckson Tada

For more: Read the blog post "What Should Our Perspective Be on Growing Older?": epm.org/growingolder

Finding Ultimate Satisfaction

When our thirst for joy is satisfied by Christ, sin becomes unattractive. Those who drink of Jesus are fully satisfied.

Ultimate satisfaction can be found only in God, the gracious Giver of all good things. We were made for Him and we will never be satisfied with less. Coming to grips with this is one of the great keys to Christian living.

When our thirst for joy is satisfied by Christ, sin becomes unattractive. We say no to the passing pleasures of immorality, not because we don't want pleasure, but because we want true pleasure, a greater and lasting pleasure found only in Christ. Those who drink of Jesus are fully satisfied (see John 6:35). We can either have our thirst quenched in Jesus, or we can plunge deeper into sin in search of what's not there.

How many times in the last twenty-four hours have you consciously looked to God and said something like "Please, my Savior, help me find in You today all that my heart longs for"? Begin today, and watch how He answers that prayer.

Perspectives from God's Word

"With you is the fountain of life; in your light do we see light" (Psalm 36:9).

"O God, you are my God, earnestly I seek you; my soul thirsts for you, my body longs for you, in a dry and weary land where there is no water" (Psalm 63:1, NIV).

Perspectives from God's People

"We are a long time in learning, that *all* our strength and salvation, is in God." —David Brainerd

"Many [people] come short, being satisfied with the works of God rather than hungering for and reaching on to God Himself." —A. W. Tozer

For more: Read the blog post "Hunger, Thirst and Craving God (Longing Part 2)": epm.org/hungerthirst

Investing—Not Just Managing—Time

*Let's wisely use the brief time
God has entrusted to us.*

We are warned to not waste our time, yet our culture encourages us to waste our lives.

Look up *TV, computer, sports radio,* and *social media* in a concordance. Not surprisingly, you won't find a single Bible verse commanding us to engage with them. But plenty of verses command us to be pure and a good manager of the life—time, abilities, money, and opportunities—God has entrusted to us. "Look carefully then how you walk, not as unwise but as wise, making the best use of the time, because the days are evil" (Ephesians 5:15–16).

Let's not squander our time. C. T. Studd said, "Only one life, 'twill soon be past, only what's done for Christ will last."

I've spent a lot of time talking to people who've been diagnosed with terminal diseases. These people, and their loved ones, have a sudden and insatiable interest in the afterlife and a desire to make their remaining time on this Earth count. Most people live unprepared for death. But those who are wise will go to a reliable source to investigate what's on the other side. They'll adjust accordingly the activities they choose during their brief stay in this world.

Perspectives from God's Word

"Teach us to number our days that we may get a heart of wisdom" (Psalm 90:12).

"Walk in wisdom toward outsiders, making the best use of the time" (Colossians 4:5).

Perspectives from God's People

"Wasting time is unbecoming a saint who is bought by the precious blood of Jesus. His time and all he has is to be used for the Lord." —George Müller

"It is impossible for a believer, no matter what his experience, to keep right with God if he will not take the trouble to spend time with God. Spend plenty of time with him; let other things go, but don't neglect Him." —J. Oswald Sanders

For more: Read the blog post "Living Life or Documenting Insignificance?": epm.org/livinglife

The Brief Window
of This Present Life

*Many Christians think and act as if there's
no eternity; we major in the momentary
and minor in the momentous.*

E arth is an in-between world touched by both Heaven and Hell. Earth leads directly into Heaven or directly into Hell, affording a choice between the two. The best of life on Earth is a glimpse of Heaven; the worst of life is a glimpse of Hell. For Christians, this present life is the closest they will come to Hell. For unbelievers, it is the closest they will come to Heaven.

Many Western Christians habitually think and act as if there is no eternity. We major in the momentary and minor in the momentous. What does God have to say about our lives here? He says this life is so brief we're like grass that grows up in the morning and wilts in the afternoon (see Isaiah 40:6–8). Our life here is but "mist that appears for a little time and then vanishes" (James 4:14).

Are you ALIVE (**A**lways **L**iving **I**n **V**iew of **E**ternity)? Are you fixing your eyes on the unseen, which is more real than anything seen? (See 2 Corinthians 4:18.)

Perspectives from God's Word

"All flesh is grass, and all its beauty is like the flower of the field. The grass withers, the flower fades" (Isaiah 40:6–7).

"Man is like a breath; his days are like a passing shadow" (Psalm 144:4).

Perspectives from God's People

"Two seconds, and we will be gone—to heaven or to hell. . . . Life is a vapor." —John Piper

"[A man's] greatest care should be for that place where he dwelleth longest; therefore eternity should be in his scope." —Thomas Manton

For more: Watch the video "Why Is It Important to Be Heavenly Minded?": epm.org/heavenlyminded

Eager Students of God's Inexhaustible Word

God expects us to study and meditate on His words, seeking to understand them—not exhaustively, but accurately.

Though we're incapable of solving the deep mysteries of God, we're fully capable of learning and appreciating more about them: "Oh, the depth of the riches and wisdom and knowledge of God! How unsearchable are his judgments and how inscrutable his ways!" (Romans 11:33).

God's thoughts are indeed higher than ours. He reduces His thoughts into words and reveals them in Scripture because He wants us to know Him. He's a good communicator and calls us to study and understand His words. "We have the mind of Christ" (1 Corinthians 2:16).

The Good News Translation renders Acts 17:11, "The people [in Berea] were more open-minded than the people in Thessalonica. They listened to the message with great eagerness, and every day they studied the Scriptures to see if what Paul said was really true." May we be like those Bereans: open minded, eager, and discerning students of the very words of God.

Perspectives from God's Word

"How great are your works, O LORD! Your thoughts are very deep!" (Psalm 92:5).

"The secret things belong to the LORD our God, but the things that are revealed belong to us and to our children forever, that we may do all the words of this law" (Deuteronomy 29:29).

Perspectives from God's People

"Remember, it is not hasty reading, but seriously meditating upon holy and heavenly truths, that makes them prove sweet and profitable to the soul." —Thomas Brooks

"The Spirit is not given to make Bible study needless, but to make it effective." —J. I. Packer

For more: Read the blog post "The Best Theological Label Is 'Berean'": epm.org/bestlabel

Representing Our
True Country

Thirsty people need us to reach out and extend
to them as cold water Christ's offer of citizenship
in another world, a coming eternal home.

There is widespread concern about many nations' economies. And widespread blame. But the problem is the human heart. What affects economics is the cumulative attributes of individuals that make up a nation: Are we marked by honesty, hard work, gratitude, and care for others, or are we obsessed with what we imagine we deserve? We can't solve all our nation's problems, but we can address the issues of our own hearts.

No matter what direction our earthly country may be going, it is our never-ending heavenly country that we should represent. Scripture says of God's people,

> They freely admitted that they lived on this earth as exiles and
> foreigners. . . . Their eyes are fixed upon their true home-land. If
> they had meant the particular country they had left behind, they
> had ample opportunity to return. No, the fact is that they longed
> for a better country altogether, nothing less than a heavenly one.
> And because of this faith of theirs, God is not ashamed to be
> called their God for in sober truth he has prepared for them a
> city in Heaven. (Hebrews 11:14–16, Phillips)

Peace, safety, and economic prosperity are threatened in the world's current crises. People living in the wreckage of this sin-stained Earth must realize that the world's main problem is its being inhabited by people like us, sinners in need of redemption. They need us to reach out our hands and extend to them, as cold water to the thirsty, Christ's offer of citizenship in another world, a coming eternal home.

Perspectives from God's Word

"How beautiful upon the mountains are the feet of him who brings good news, who publishes peace, who brings good news of happiness, who publishes salvation, who says to Zion, 'Your God reigns'" (Isaiah 52:7).

"In this tent we groan, longing to put on our heavenly dwelling. . . . While we are at home in the body we are away from the Lord. . . . We would rather be away from the body and at home with the Lord" (2 Corinthians 5:2, 6, 8).

Perspectives from God's People

"Our deepest instinct is heaven. Heaven is the ache in our bones, the splinter in our heart." —Mark Buchanan

"I must keep alive in myself the desire for my true country, which I shall not find till after death." —C. S. Lewis

For more: Read the article "Dual Citizenship": epm.org/citizenship

The Courage to Follow Him

When we follow the Lord wherever
He leads, we can depend upon Him to
give us courage to take the next step.

It's not always pleasant to talk about the issues God's Word addresses. When I meditate on Scripture, it's very common for me to feel uncomfortable about what I'm reading. But to follow Christ is not about being comfortable. It's about being sold out to the God with the nail-scarred hands—being radical for Him, standing up for Him, and speaking the truth in love, with grace.

When we follow the Lord wherever He leads, we can then depend upon Him to give us more courage to take the next step. "If anyone serves me, he must follow me; and where I am, there will my servant be also. If anyone serves me, the Father will honor him" (John 12:26).

An old poem, which Elisabeth Elliot loved to quote, says,

Do it immediately; do it with prayer;
Do it reliantly, casting all care;
Do it with reverence, tracing His hand
Who placed it before thee with earnest command,
Stayed on Omnipotence, safe 'neath His wing,
Leave all resultings. Do THE NEXT THING.[8]

Christ promises that anything we lose while taking that next, courageous step in humble service to Him, we will regain a trillion times over in the long tomorrow (see Matthew 19:29).

Perspectives from God's Word

"If anyone would come after me, let him deny himself and take up his cross daily and follow me. For whoever would save his life will lose it, but whoever loses his life for my sake will save it" (Luke 9:23–24).

"Be strong in the Lord and in the strength of his might" (Ephesians 6:10).

Perspectives from God's People

"Courage is almost a contradiction in terms. It means a strong desire to live taking the form of a readiness to die." —G. K. Chesterton

"It is easier to find a score of men wise enough to discover the truth than to find one intrepid enough, in the face of opposition, to stand up for it." —A. A. Hodge

For more: Read the blog post "How Does One Gain the Courage to Make Personal Sacrifices for God?": epm.org/courage

The Ultimate
Restoration

God is the ultimate salvage artist. He loves to
restore things and make them even better.

Because Earth is the realm where God's glory has been the most challenged and resisted, it is also the stage on which His glory will be the most graphically demonstrated. By reclaiming, restoring, and resurrecting Earth—and empowering a regenerated humanity to reign over it—God will accomplish His purpose of bringing glory to Himself. "Of the increase of his government and of peace there will be no end" (Isaiah 9:7).

A great year-round song is "Joy to the World," because it looks forward to Christ's return and the New Earth. "No more let sins and sorrows grow. . . . / He comes to make his blessings flow / far as the curse is found." Christ's redemptive work will reverse the Curse and restore the Earth (see 2 Peter 3:13).

If God had wanted to, He could have consigned Adam and Eve to Hell and started over. Instead, He chose to redeem what He started with—the heavens, Earth, and humanity—to bring them back to His original purpose. God is the ultimate salvage artist. He loves to restore things and make them even better. His perfect plan is "to unite all things in him, things in heaven and things on earth" (Ephesians 1:10).

Perspectives from God's Word

"[Jesus] must remain in heaven until the time comes for God to restore everything, as he promised long ago through his holy prophets" (Acts 3:21, NIV).

"In the new world, when the Son of Man will sit on his glorious throne, you who have followed me will also sit on twelve thrones, judging the twelve tribes of Israel" (Matthew 19:28).

Perspectives from God's People

"The kingdom of God . . . does not mean merely the salvation of certain individuals nor even the salvation of a chosen group of people. It means nothing less than the complete renewal of the entire cosmos, culminating in the new heaven and the new earth." —Anthony Hoekema

"Our Lord has written the promise of the resurrection, not in books alone, but in every leaf in spring-time." —Martin Luther

For more: Read the blog post "Eagerly Anticipating the New Heavens to Come": epm.org/newheavens

Striving to Be a Faithful Steward

Stewardship is about time, abilities, relationships, work; it's not only about money. It is the whole Christian life.

A steward's primary goal is to be "found faithful" by his master. He proves himself faithful by wisely using the master's resources to accomplish the tasks delegated to him. Those resources include not only money but time, gifting, relationships, employment. From this perspective, stewardship isn't a narrow subcategory of the Christian life. On the contrary, stewardship is the Christian life.

God says, "It is required of stewards that they be found faithful," not successful (1 Corinthians 4:2). We must leave the results to Him. Jesus said, "For where your treasure is, there will your heart be also" (Luke 12:34). The more we invest in the things that matter to God, the more our hearts are drawn to Him. The person who puts his treasures into God's hands demonstrates love for God and others. Since his heart will follow his treasures, not only are the lives of the needy changed by his giving but also his own.

God pays a great deal of attention to the "little things." He cares for the lilies of the field, is concerned with the fall of a single sparrow, and numbers the hairs on our heads (see Matthew 6:28; 10:29, 30). As a business owner pays attention to how an employee handles the little things, God pays attention to us. What we do with a little time, a little talent, and a little money tells God a lot.

Perspectives from God's Word

"If then you have not been faithful in the unrighteous wealth, who will entrust to you the true riches?" (Luke 16:11).

"[The nobleman] said to [his servant], 'Well done, good servant! Because you have been faithful in a very little, you shall have authority over ten cities'" (Luke 19:17).

Perspectives from God's People

"The world asks, *what* does a man own? Christ, *how* does he use it?" —Andrew Murray

"All that we have is a loan from God: we are God's stewards; we are God's debtors. Let this thought sink down deeply in our hearts." —J. C. Ryle

For more: Read the blog post "A Man from Heaven: How Would He Spend His Money?": epm.org/manfromheaven

Finding True Contentment

The way to contentment in each season of life is to choose to see the advantages of our present calling.

E ach phase of life is different, with its own challenges but also its own rewards. The way to contentment is to see the advantages of our present calling and to trust God's purposes in our circumstances.

Scottish theologian Sinclair Ferguson writes, "Christian contentment . . . is the direct fruit of having no higher ambition than to belong to the Lord and to be totally at His disposal in the place He appoints, at the time He chooses, with the provision He is pleased to make."[9]

We won't be fully content until we're home with our Beloved. The closest we can get to contentment—and to Heaven—while we're still here as aliens and strangers on this Earth, is when we come away with Jesus and get away from His substitutes. We need to tear down the idols and give God sole occupation of the throne of our lives. "Little children, keep yourselves from idols" (1 John 5:21). True contentment comes when we're looking to only one God, the genuine article.

Perspectives from God's Word

"Godliness with contentment is great gain" (1 Timothy 6:6).

"For the sake of Christ, then, I am content with weaknesses, insults, hardships, persecutions, and calamities. For when I am weak, then I am strong" (2 Corinthians 12:10).

Perspectives from God's People

"Contentment is one of the flowers of heaven, and, if we would have it, it must be cultivated." —Charles Spurgeon

"If the sun of God's countenance shine upon me, I may well be content to be wet with some rain of affliction." —Joseph Hall

For more: Read the blog post "The Joy and Happiness of Giving Thanks in Every Circumstance": epm.org/everycircumstance

Pursuing the Right Perspective

We can and should live now with the perspective that will be ours one minute after we die.

Jesus calls His followers citizens of Heaven. When we think more about dinner out tomorrow than the banquet on the New Earth with Abraham, Isaac, and Jacob, we lose sight of Heaven and surrender the present joy that comes in anticipating it. We must fix our eyes on things that, for the present, remain invisible.

Immediately upon leaving this world, all who know Christ will gain the right perspective. The good news is we don't have to wait until then. We can and should live now with the perspective that will be ours one minute after we die.

Paul's admonition in Colossians 3:1 is to diligently, actively, single-mindedly pursue the things above: in other words, Jesus and Heaven. Don't just have a conversation, read a book, or listen to a sermon, then feel as if you've fulfilled the command. If you're going to spend the next lifetime living in Heaven, why not spend this lifetime anticipating and preparing for Heaven?

Perspectives from God's Word

"Set your minds on things that are above, not on things that are on earth" (Colossians 3:2).

"Since you are waiting for these [the New Heavens and New Earth], be diligent to be found by him without spot or blemish, and at peace" (2 Peter 3:14).

Perspectives from God's People

"It becomes us to spend this life only as a journey towards heaven. . . . Why should we labour for, or set our hearts on, any thing else, but that which is our proper end, and true happiness?" —Jonathan Edwards

"The consideration of heaven is no mere spiritual luxury, no mere intellectual dissipation, no imaginative reverie, but is really and definitely practical and suitable . . . and has real bearing on our daily life." —W. H. Griffith Thomas

For more: Read the blog post "Why an Eternal Perspective Changes Everything": epm.org/changes

Trusting the Author
of the Story

God writes conflict into our lives
not just to make His redemptive
story better but to make us better.

I've written seven full-length novels and some shorter works of fiction. My central characters always face great turmoil, uncertainty, and suffering. Were I to write a novel about lives without conflict, where characters get everything they want, nobody would read it. Their suffering creates a far richer and deeper story.

So who am I to say that God shouldn't write such things into *His* story, including my part?

The Author of life has placed us in a story far bigger than ourselves. We can trust God not only to bring the whole story together but also to do with our parts of it what He knows to be best. (It may help if we remind ourselves that Jesus is both the author and the main character, while the rest of us are in supporting roles.)

God loves a great story, and we who know Him will recall and celebrate His story for all eternity. Before we fault Him for the plot twists we don't like, we should remember that Jesus has written this story in His own blood. Though all the characters will suffer, none suffers as much as He did or for a greater purpose.

Perspectives from God's Word

"Joseph said to his brothers, . . . 'Do not be angry with yourselves for selling me here, because it was to save lives that God sent me ahead of you. . . . So then, it was not you who sent me here, but God'" (Genesis 45:4-5, 8, NIV).

"In your book were written, every one of them, the days that were formed for me, when as yet there was none of them" (Psalm 139:16).

Perspectives from God's People

"When a train goes through a tunnel and it gets dark, you don't throw away the ticket and jump off. You sit still and trust the engineer." —Corrie ten Boom

"I have often imagined my own story fitting into some greater scheme, the half of which I may never fathom. I simply do not see the bigger picture, but I *choose to believe* that there is a bigger picture and that my loss is part of some wonderful story authored by God himself." —Jerry Sittser

For more: Read the article "If You Were the Author, How Would You Have Written the Story?": epm.org/authorstory

Present Suffering, Future Perspective

We are to rejoice in our inheritance in Heaven even as God sovereignly uses difficulties in our lives as a fire to refine, purify, and strengthen our faith.

'll never forget my first thirty seconds of high school. I walked in the front door, tripped, and fell on my face . . . right in front of three cheerleaders. They laughed hysterically. Not a good start for a freshman desperately wanting to be cool!

At the time, that incident hurt worse than a serious ankle injury I suffered while playing football. Fast-forward forty years, and though I still remember it vividly, my past embarrassment doesn't hurt a bit. Now I laugh. Of course, my teenage troubles do *not* compare to having cancer, being tortured, or seeing a child die. I only mean that certain experiences that bring us genuine pain no longer do so as time passes and we gain perspective.

God promises that our future with Him will break forth in such glorious happiness that all present suffering will pale in comparison (see Romans 8:18; 2 Corinthians 4:17). *All* who know Jesus will have a happy ending. We just haven't seen it yet.

Perspectives from God's Word

"These [trials] have come so that your faith—of greater worth than gold, which perishes even though refined by fire—may be proved genuine and may result in praise, glory and honor when Jesus Christ is revealed" (1 Peter 1:6–7, NIV).

"Count it all joy, my brothers, when you meet trials of various kinds, for you know that the testing of your faith produces steadfastness" (James 1:2–3).

Perspectives from God's People

"Everything is necessary that God sends our way; nothing can be necessary that He withholds." —John Newton

"How often do we resist the circumstances that God's using to teach us dependence on Him?" —Nancy DeMoss Wolgemuth

For more: Read the blog post "Turning Bad into Best": epm.org/badbest

Homesick for Eden's Happiness

When we separate God from happiness
and from our longing for happiness,
we undermine the Christian worldview.

B ased on books I've read, sermons I've heard, and conversations I've had, I'm convinced that many Christians believe our desire for happiness doesn't come from God but was birthed in humanity's fall into sin.

Were we merely the product of natural selection and survival of the fittest, we'd have no grounds for believing any ancient happiness existed. But even those who have never been taught about the Fall and the Curse intuitively know that something has gone seriously wrong.

Why else would we long for happiness and sense what a utopian society should look like if we've never seen one? We are nostalgic for an Eden we've only heard echoes of. What if God made us for happiness, and therefore our desire to be happy is inseparable from our longing for God? What if He wired His image bearers for happiness before sin entered the world, and what if that wiring can be properly directed at Him and all He wants for us? How might this perspective change our approach to life, parenting, church, ministry, business, sports, entertainment, and everything else?

Perspectives from God's Word

"Let everything that breathes sing praises to the LORD! Praise the LORD!" (Psalm 150:6, NLT).

"Satisfy us in the morning with your steadfast love, that we may rejoice and be glad all our days" (Psalm 90:14).

Perspectives from God's People

"Happiness is what all mankind want to obtain: the desire of it is deeply planted in the human heart." —J. C. Ryle

"It is as natural for the reasonable creature to desire to be happy, as it is for the fire to burn." —Thomas Manton

For more: Read the blog post "Why Does Everyone Want to Be Happy?": epm.org/wanthappy

Forgiveness Sets Us Free

When we refuse to forgive others, we inflict the greatest damage on ourselves.

I've seen families, friends, neighbors, and churches torn apart by the refusal to forgive. If we believe in the joy-giving power of forgiveness, it will transform our perspectives and help us live happier, more God-honoring lives.

Every one of us could call up a catalog of grievances done to us by our children, parents, friends, spouses, employers, neighbors, the DMV, or the IRS. Some wrongs are real and serious, others are imaginary or exaggerated, but *all can undermine happiness* . . . unless true forgiveness is demonstrated by our refusal to rehearse those wrongs.

People who "pay back" family and friends with unforgiveness don't realize they inflict the greatest damage on themselves. The saying is true: "Bitterness is like drinking poison and waiting for the other person to die." Lewis Smedes wrote, "When we forgive, we set a prisoner free and discover that the prisoner we set free is us."[10]

Perspectives from God's Word

"Bear with each other and forgive whatever grievances you may have against one another. Forgive as the Lord forgave you" (Colossians 3:13, NIV).

"Whenever you stand praying, forgive, if you have anything against anyone, so that your Father also who is in heaven may forgive you your trespasses" (Mark 11:25).

Perspectives from God's People

"The grace we receive in forgiveness gives us the grace to be forgiving." —Philip Graham Ryken

"Forgiveness is the only way to not be kidnapped by the past. It is the only way to give your relationships the blessing of fresh starts and new beginnings." —Paul Tripp

For more: Read the blog post "The Joy of Forgiveness": epm.org/joyforgiveness

God's Future Dwelling Place

Heaven, by definition, is God's special
dwelling place. We're told that one day "the
dwelling of God" will be with mankind on Earth.

Wherever God chooses to put His throne is Heaven. He has revealed that He will relocate His central dwelling from the place we now call Heaven to the New Earth to live with His risen people (see Revelation 21:3). When He puts His kingdom throne on the New Earth (see 22:3), it will transform that world into Heaven.

Jesus says of anyone who would be His disciple, "My Father will love [the one who keeps my word], and we will come to him and make our home with him" (John 14:23). This is a picture of God's ultimate plan: not to take us up to live in a realm made for Him but to join us in the realm He made for us.

When Jesus Christ came to Earth, one of the names given to Him was Immanuel, which means "God with us." The Incarnation means that God became man and lived with us. And when Jesus ascended to Heaven in His resurrected body, it demonstrated that the Incarnation wasn't temporary but permanent. This has great bearing on where God might choose for us and Him to dwell together. The New Earth will be Heaven incarnate, just as Jesus Christ is God incarnate.

Perspectives from God's Word

"I saw the holy city, new Jerusalem, coming down out of heaven from God, prepared as a bride adorned for her husband. And I heard a loud voice from the throne saying, 'Behold, the dwelling place of God is with man. He will dwell with them, and they will be his people, and God himself will be with them as their God" (Revelation 21:2–3).

"The throne of God and of the Lamb will be in the city, and his servants will serve him" (Revelation 22:3, NIV).

Perspectives from God's People

"Christians long for the fulfillment of Emmanuel. . . . We don't hope merely for the day when we go to live with God, but ultimately for that final day when God comes to live with us." —Michael Wittmer

"God's glory will fill and permeate the *entire* new Heaven— not just one centralized place. Thus, wherever we go in Heaven, we will be in the immediate presence of the full glory of God." —Steven J. Lawson

For more: Read the blog post "What's the Difference Between the Present Heaven and the Future Heaven?": epm.org/futureheaven

The Promise of Great Reward

For those who have served Christ faithfully, the judgment seat will be a time of commendation and celebration.

A day of judgment is coming upon all men. God promises great reward for all who have served Him faithfully. He will reward every loyal servant for works done in this life: "At that time each will receive his praise from God" (1 Corinthians 4:5, NIV). This is a particularly encouraging passage, suggesting that God will find something to praise and reward each one of us for. Shouldn't that motivate us to do more for our Father that He will take pleasure in and be proud of?

God rewards generously, promising a return of "a hundredfold" (Matthew 19:29). This is ten thousand percent interest, a return far out of proportion to the amount invested. No earthly investment will pay such dividends, and even if it did, they wouldn't last.

God is for us, not against us (see Romans 8:31). He doesn't want the works of our lifetime to go up in smoke. He wants us to have eternal rewards, and He has given us every resource in Christ to live the godly life that will result in those eternal rewards (see 1 Corinthians 3:12–15; 2 Peter 1:3).

Perspectives from God's Word

"Whatever good anyone does, this he will receive back from the Lord, whether he is a bondservant or is free" (Ephesians 6:8).

"He will render to each one according to his works" (Romans 2:6).

Perspectives from God's People

"It is my happiness that I have served Him who never fails to reward His servants to the full extent of His promise."
—John Calvin

"He who provides for this life, but takes no care for eternity, is wise for a moment, but a fool forever." —John Tillotson

For More: Read the blog post "Motivated by Eternal Reward?": epm.org/motivatedreward

King over All, Including the Weather

*Human arrogance daily makes foolish
claims that beg to be disproved.*

In 1815 a confident Napoleon Bonaparte determined where and
when to advance against the British. He chose Waterloo as the
place and June 18 as the day, believing England would be at France's
feet by battle's end. But it was not to be, and historians believe rain
was one of the factors that dramatically affected the outcome.

The prophet Jeremiah asked, "Are there any among the false
gods of the nations that can bring rain? Or can the heavens give
showers? Are you not he, O LORD our God?" (Jeremiah 14:22).
Rain is one of countless thousands of small things that God can
use to His ends, usually in ways unknown to us. (One of the pleasures of eternity may be God revealing to us His hidden purposes,
which will give us an inside look into human history.)

Many centuries before Napoleon, another arrogant ruler, Nebuchadnezzar, made a humbling discovery. God promised to take
Nebuchadnezzar's kingdom from him for a time, telling him,
"Your kingdom will be restored to you when you acknowledge that
Heaven rules" (Daniel 4:26, NIV). That's exactly what happened,
and the thoroughly chastened king afterward insisted that God
"does as he pleases with the powers of heaven and the peoples of the

earth. No one can hold back his hand or say to him: 'What have you done?'" (verse 35, NIV).

Perspectives from God's Word

"I am God, and there is no other; I am God, and there is none like me" (Isaiah 46:9).

"Whatever the LORD pleases, he does, in heaven and on earth, in the seas and all deeps" (Psalm 135:6).

Perspectives from God's People

"Cheer up, Christian! Things are not left to chance: no blind fate rules the world. God hath purposes, and those purposes are fulfilled. God hath plans, and those plans are wise, and never can be dislocated." —Charles Spurgeon

"Divine sovereignty is not the sovereignty of a tyrannical Despot, but the exercised pleasure of One who is infinitely wise and good!" —A. W. Pink

For more: Read the blog post "The Beautiful Intertwining of God's Sovereignty and Human Free Will": epm.org/intertwining

Sovereign over Good and Evil

*Without God's permission,
Satan has no power to act.*

Though evil had no part in God's original creation, it was part of His original plan, because *redemption* from evil was part of His plan. Before He created the world, He knew evil would come, and He used it to play its necessary role.

Scripture doesn't distance God from disasters and secondary evils the way His children often do. Rather, He says unapologetically, "I form the light and create darkness, I bring prosperity and create disaster; I, the LORD, do all these things" (Isaiah 45:7, NIV).

Satan may bring about a "natural" disaster, but the book of Job makes clear that God continues to reign, even while selectively allowing Satan to do evil things. Satan knew that without God's explicit permission, he had no authority to incite humans to do evil, to bring down lightning to cause fires, or to send the wind to blow down a building and take lives. We should know this too. Satan is a lion, yes, but a lion on God's leash.

Perspectives from God's Word

"Does disaster come to a city, unless the LORD has done it?" (Amos 3:6).

"He is unchangeable, and who can turn him back? What he desires, that he does" (Job 23:13).

Perspectives from God's People

"We dread the sovereignty of man, because we have no security of its being exercised in mercy, or even in justice: we rejoice in the sovereignty of God, because we are sure it is always exercised for the good of his people."
—Alexander Carson

"Confidence in the sovereignty of God in *all* that affects us is crucial to our trusting Him." —Jerry Bridges

For more: Read the article "God's and Humanity's Roles in Natural Disasters": epm.org/naturaldisasters

What We're Really Longing For

*We may imagine we want a
thousand different things, but God
is the One we really long for.*

O God, you are my God, earnestly I seek you; my soul thirsts for you, my body longs for you, in a dry and weary land where there is no water" (Psalm 63:1, NIV). We may imagine we want a thousand different things, but God is the One we really long for. His presence brings satisfaction; His absence brings thirst and longing.

Asaph says, "Whom have I in heaven but you? And earth has nothing I desire besides you" (Psalm 73:25, NIV). This may seem an overstatement: There's nothing on Earth this man desires but God? But he's affirming that the central desire of our hearts is for God. No matter what we think we're searching for, God is whom we truly hope to find. Augustine prayed, "You have made us for Yourself, and our hearts are restless until they find their rest in You."[11]

When we see Him with our resurrected eyes, we will realize that all our lives, as we went down every dead-end street pursuing what we thought we wanted, it was really Him we were longing for.

Perspectives from God's Word

"As a deer pants for flowing streams, so pants my soul for you, O God. My soul thirsts for God, for the living God" (Psalm 42:1-2).

"Yet in my flesh I shall see God, whom I shall see for myself, and my eyes shall behold, and not another. My heart faints within me!" (Job 19:26-27).

Perspectives from God's People

"How sweet all at once it was for me to be rid of those fruitless joys which I had once feared to lose! . . . You drove them from me, you who are the true, the sovereign joy. You drove them from me and took their place, you who are sweeter than all pleasure." —Augustine

"Christ is the desire of nations, the joy of angels, the delight of the Father. What solace, then, must that soul be filled with, which hath the possession of Christ to all eternity!" —John Bunyan

For more: Read the blog post "Longings of the Heart": epm.org/longings

The Deadly
Life of Ease

*Jesus isn't our gofer who exists to
run our errands. Rather, He is our
Sovereign who gives us what we need
while sometimes denying what we want.*

We want deliverance from suffering. We want our loved ones to be protected. We don't want economic crises, job losses, car accidents, or cancer. Our prayers and often our expectations boil down to this: Jesus should make our lives go smoothly. That's what we want in a Messiah. But it is not what God wants.

Jesus is not our personal assistant charged with granting our wishes. While He doesn't always give us what we want, He always gives us what we need.

Ironically, the life of ease we most desire is the very kind of life that would make us the people we least admire. Because, let's be honest, virtually everyone who has suffered little in life is shallow, unmotivated, self-absorbed, and lacking in character. You know it and so do I. And yet we do everything we can to avoid challenges, both to our children and to ourselves.

God's parenting method doesn't shield us from adversity and the character it builds. He knows the life of ease is deadly to the development of Christlike character.

Perspectives from God's Word

"And we, who with unveiled faces all reflect the Lord's glory, are being transformed into his likeness with ever-increasing glory, which comes from the Lord, who is the Spirit" (2 Corinthians 3:18, NIV).

"For those God foreknew he also predestined to be conformed to the likeness of his Son, that he might be the firstborn among many brothers" (Romans 8:29, NIV).

Perspectives from God's People

"Jesus, you are righteousness, not my moral coach; my Lord, not my co-pilot; my life, not my concierge."
—Scotty Ward Smith

"If your hope is anchored in Jesus, the worst case future scenario for you is resurrection and everlasting life."
—Scott Sauls

For more: Read the blog post "God Doesn't Love Us on Our Preferred Terms, but on His Own": epm.org/histerms

The Joy of Self-Forgetfulness

*Self-obsession is a formula
for unhappiness.*

When I meditate on Christ's unfathomable love and grace, I lose myself in Him, and before I know it, I'm happy. But when I focus on my problems and especially how badly others are treating me (or so I imagine), happiness flies away.

C. S. Lewis said of the humble person, "He will not be thinking about humility: he will not be thinking about himself at all."[12] Tim Keller says, "Gospel-humility is not needing to think about myself. . . . I stop connecting every experience, every conversation, with myself. . . . The freedom of self-forgetfulness."[13]

When we lose ourselves in God's purposes, Jesus says we'll find ourselves—and also eternal life, and therefore great joy (see John 12:25). The "sacrifice" of following Jesus produces in us the greatest, most lasting happiness.

Perspectives from God's Word

"Whoever finds his life will lose it, and whoever loses his life for my sake will find it" (Matthew 10:39).

"Oh come, let us worship and bow down; let us kneel before the LORD, our Maker!" (Psalm 95:6).

Perspectives from God's People

"We cannot make much of ourselves and much of the Lord Jesus Christ simultaneously." —Alistair Begg

"Humility is fundamentally a form of self-forgetfulness as opposed to pride's self-fixation. Humility can set you free because when you think about yourself less you are free to think about Christ more." —Jason Meyer

For more: Read the blog post "A Life of Humility": epm.org/lifehumility

The Good News of Happiness

The gospel is the best news there has ever been or ever will be.

When we hear good news, what's our reaction? Happiness, excitement, delight, and celebration, right? The greater the news, the greater the happiness. The good news is a concrete, reality-grounded call to happiness: Jesus really did become a man, go to the cross, and rise from the grave. He truly is with us now and will return one day. These facts separate the gospel from wishful thinking.

The gospel is very much about happiness. Delivery from eternal damnation is delivery from eternal misery. What better qualifies as the "good news of happiness" (Isaiah 52:7)? What better sums up God's gifts of goodness, loving-kindness, grace, mercy, salvation, rebirth, renewal, and the indwelling Holy Spirit (see Titus 3:5–7) than the word *happiness*?

What if we spread the extraordinarily good news of Jesus by offering people the happiness they long for? Imagine if churches were known as communities of Jesus-centered happiness, overflowing with the sheer gladness of what it means to live out the good news!

Perspectives from God's Word

"The angel said to them, 'Fear not, for behold, I bring you good news of great joy that will be for all the people'" (Luke 2:10).

"I came that they may have life and have it abundantly" (John 10:10).

Perspectives from God's People

"'Evangelion' (that we call the gospel) is a Greek word, and signifies good, merry, glad and joyful tidings, that makes a man's heart glad, and makes him sing, dance, and leap for joy." —William Tyndale

"I assert without hesitation, that the conversion described in Scripture is a happy thing and not a miserable one. . . . I am confident the converted man is the happiest man." —J. C. Ryle

For more: Read the blog post "Teach Your Children About the Happy God": epm.org/childrenhappy

Suffering's Painful, Beautiful Benefits

The Master Artist chose us, the flawed and unusable, to be crafted into the image of Christ and fulfill our destiny in displaying Jesus to the watching universe.

For most of us it takes the chiseling effect of loss, hardship, sickness, and even tragedy before we adequately recognize and admit our true weakness, and therefore our need for God. The same is true for our becoming more grateful, more humble, and more God-focused. Over time, the experience of suffering can make us spiritually stronger, more dependent upon God, and less fearful.

It can also increase our effectiveness in talking to others about Christ. People recognize the power of the gospel when they hear it from those who've suffered yet retained their faith. No wonder the Bible tells us to "consider it pure joy . . . whenever you face trials of many kinds" (James 1:2, NIV).

Those who embrace the Christian faith most deeply and passionately are usually not those enjoying comfort and ease, but those who live with suffering. Many people who have endured deep hardship turn toward God in their suffering, having found that nothing else can bear the weight of their trust.

Perspectives from God's Word

"We were so utterly burdened beyond our strength that we despaired of life itself. . . . But that was to make us rely not on ourselves but on God who raises the dead" (2 Corinthians 1:8–9).

"We rejoice in our sufferings, knowing that suffering produces endurance, and endurance produces character, and character produces hope" (Romans 5:3–4).

Perspectives from God's People

"Winter prepares the earth for the spring, so do afflictions, sanctified, prepare the soul for glory." —Richard Sibbes

"The secret formula of the saints: When I am in the cellar of affliction, I look for the Lord's choicest wines." —Samuel Rutherford

For more: Read the blog post "Crisis and Tragedy": epm.org/crisis-tragedy

Humble Savior, Sent to Earth

*Long before His crucifixion, Jesus Christ
endured countless indignities on Earth.*

In the Old Testament, we read how God kept reaching down to His people. "The LORD . . . sent word to them through his messengers again and again. . . . But they mocked God's messengers" (2 Chronicles 36:15–16, NIV).

Finally God sent His Son to Earth. He came in humiliation; many imagined He was conceived out of wedlock, a shameful thing in that era. He grew up in a town of ill repute: "Nazareth! Can anything good come from there?" (John 1:46, NIV). He worked as a humble carpenter, lived in relative poverty, and endured many indignities as He spent three years in ministry, teaching and healing and speaking the good news of God's kingdom.

When I first read this story as an unbeliever— having been raised with no knowledge of God—part of what drew me to Christ is how the gospel accounts seem so contrary to typical human reasoning, yet I found them completely credible. No human would make up such a story! It had the ring of truth to me . . . and still does.

Does Christ's redemptive work for you resonate in your heart and mind? How does it make you feel and think?

Perspectives from God's Word

"He had no beauty or majesty to attract us to him,
nothing in his appearance that we should desire him"
(Isaiah 53:2, NIV).

"Have this mind among yourselves, which is yours in Christ
Jesus, who, though he was in the form of God, did not count
equality with God a thing to be grasped, but emptied
himself, by taking the form of a servant" (Philippians 2:5–7).

Perspectives from God's People

"There has never been a greater humiliation of a person
than that of Jesus. No one has ever descended so low
because no one has ever come from so high." —Mark Jones

"Because we children of Adam want to become great,
He became small. Because we will not stoop, He humbled
Himself. Because we want to rule, He came to serve."
—J. Oswald Sanders

For more: Read the article "God with Us": epm.org/withus

The Incomparable Beauty of Purity

To embrace purity is to lay claim to a magnificent gift. Purity creates beauty that will never end.

Sexual purity is not an option for an obedient Christian; it's a requirement. God's will is centered on our character and moral purity much more than on our circumstances, such as job, housing, and schooling. Want to know God's will? You don't have to wonder: "It is God's will that you should be sanctified: that you should avoid sexual immorality" (1 Thessalonians 4:3, NIV).

When God calls on us to pursue purity, He's not telling us to abandon joy. In fact, He is inviting us to choose what will bring us the greatest joy!

To embrace purity is to lay claim to a magnificent gift. Purity is incomparably beautiful, like the fragrance of a rose after a summer shower. And it's a beauty that will never end, because all who live in Heaven will be pure: "Nothing impure will ever enter it, nor will anyone who does what is shameful or deceitful, but only those whose names are written in the Lamb's book of life" (Revelation 21:27, NIV).

Perspectives from God's Word

"The fear of the LORD is a fountain of life, that one may turn away from the snares of death" (Proverbs 14:27).

"Put to death therefore what is earthly in you: sexual immorality, impurity, passion, evil desire, and covetousness, which is idolatry. On account of these the wrath of God is coming. In these you too once walked, when you were living in them" (Colossians 3:5–7).

Perspectives from God's People

"Either sin will keep you from the Word, or the Word will keep you from sin." —John Bunyan

"Little souls make little lusts have great power. The soul, as it were, expands to encompass the magnitude of its treasure. The human soul was made to see and savor the supremacy of Christ. Nothing else is big enough to enlarge the soul as God intended and make little lusts lose their power." —John Piper

For more: Read the blog post "How Do You Define Purity?": epm.org/definepurity

The Universe's Greatest Tragedy

The most basic truth is that there are only two possible destinations after death: Heaven and Hell.

If we understood Hell even the slightest bit, none of us would ever say, "Go to Hell." It is far too easy to go to Hell. It requires no change of course, no navigational adjustments. We were born with our autopilot set toward Hell. It is nothing to take lightly; Hell is the single greatest tragedy in the universe.

Many people define *love* by whatever sounds nice or feels good, while God loves us enough to tell us the truth—there are two eternal destinations, not one, and we must choose the right path if we are to go to Heaven. All roads do not lead to Heaven. Only one does: Jesus Christ. He said, "No one comes to the Father except through me" (John 14:6). All other roads lead to Hell.

The high stakes involved in the choice between Heaven and Hell will cause us to appreciate Heaven in deeper ways, never taking it for granted and always praising God for His grace that forever delivers us *from* what we deserve and delivers us *to* what we don't deserve.

Perspectives from God's Word

"God presented [Jesus] as a sacrifice of atonement, through faith in his blood" (Romans 3:25, NIV).

"This is the testimony: God has given us eternal life, and this life is in his Son. He who has the Son has life; he who does not have the Son of God does not have life" (1 John 5:11–12, NIV).

Perspectives from God's People

"The safest road to Hell is the gradual one—the gentle slope, soft underfoot, without sudden turnings, without milestones, without signposts." —C. S. Lewis

"My memory is nearly gone, but I remember two things: That I am a great sinner, and that Christ is a great Savior." —John Newton

For more: Read the blog post "Does Being Like Jesus Mean Not Talking About Hell?": epm.org/talkabouthell

Letting God's Words Shape Ours

To have lasting value and impact, our words must be touched and shaped by God's words.

The power of the words we speak is far greater than we realize. "Death and life are in the power of the tongue" (Proverbs 18:21).

God gives us no task to accomplish except those that require our dependence on Him. Therefore, there is nothing we should regard as automatic. No conversation should be on autopilot. We need to ask for His guidance, His wisdom, and His empowerment so our words please Him and so we will not have to account for careless words on the Day of Judgment.

If we want our words to have lasting value and impact, they need to be touched and shaped by God's words. That will happen as we make ongoing daily choices to expose our minds to Scripture, to meet with Christ, and to let Him rub off on us.

Perspectives from God's Word

"I tell you, on the day of judgment people will give account for every careless word they speak" (Matthew 12:36).

"So shall my word be that goes out from my mouth; it shall not return to me empty, but it shall accomplish that which I purpose, and shall succeed in the thing for which I sent it" (Isaiah 55:11).

Perspectives from God's People

"An unbridled tongue is . . . the chariot of the Devil, wherein he rides in triumph." —Edward Reyner

"God has given us two ears, but one tongue, to show that we should be swift to hear, but slow to speak. God has set a double fence before the tongue, the teeth, and the lips, to teach us to be wary that we offend not with our tongue." —Thomas Watson

For more: Read the article "Biblical Principles for Godly Verbal Communication": epm.org/communication

Our Future Reign Under Christ

Christ will restore us to the thrones
occupied so briefly by Adam and Eve.
He will hand over to us the Kingdom.

The Bible's central story line revolves around a question: Who will reign over Earth? Because it is the realm where God's glory has been most challenged and resisted, it is therefore also the stage on which His glory will be most graphically demonstrated. By reclaiming, restoring, renewing, and resurrecting Earth, and empowering a regenerated humanity to reign over it, God will accomplish His purpose of bringing glory to Himself.

God's claim to His throne is absolute. The claim of human beings to their thrones is valid *only* if they remain in submission to God, who delegated dominion to them as His heirs and sub-rulers. Satan's claim to the throne is false.

Ultimately, Satan will be eternally dethroned and God will be permanently enthroned. Christ will become the unchallenged, absolute Ruler of the universe and then will turn over to His Father the Kingdom He has won (see 1 Corinthians 15:28). Redeemed humans will be God's unchallenged, delegated rulers of the New Earth. God and humanity will live together in eternal happiness, forever deepening their relationships, as the glory of God permeates every aspect of the new creation.

Perspectives from God's Word

"Then the sovereignty, power and greatness of the kingdoms under the whole heaven will be handed over to the saints, the people of the Most High" (Daniel 7:27, NIV).

"Having disarmed the powers and authorities, [Christ] made a public spectacle of them, triumphing over them by the cross" (Colossians 2:15, NIV).

Perspectives from God's People

"Can you imagine living in a society where everyone is so happy with leadership decisions, they rejoice and celebrate? Can you imagine a world where no one ever again complains about government? Yes, it's possible! It's predicted. It's prepared. It's the kingdom of heaven. And it's real!"
—Larry Dick

"Our lives now are shaping us and preparing us for a future rule, and that includes the honing of a conscience and a sense of wisdom and prudence and justice. God is teaching us, as he taught our Lord, to learn in little things how to be in charge of great things." —Russell Moore

For more: Read the blog post "God's Kingdom . . . and Ours": epm.org/kingdom

Who You Are
in the Dark

*Character is what you are in the dark
when no one but God can see you.*

Image is how we look on the outside. Character is who we are in private, when no one but God can see us. Character is who we really are. "All a man's ways seem innocent to him, but motives are weighed by the LORD" (Proverbs 16:2, NIV).

Anyone can look good in front of an audience or even in front of friends. It's an entirely different thing to stand naked before God, to be known as you truly are on the inside. How desperately we need His saving grace!

"His divine power has granted to us all things that pertain to life and godliness" (2 Peter 1:3). In light of what is ours in Christ, Peter says in verse 5 that we should "make every effort" to cultivate Christlike character and habits. So if God has already given us everything we need in Christ, shouldn't we invest our lives in Spirit-empowered service for the love of God and others, living for the day when we'll stand before His throne?

Perspectives from God's Word

"All the ways of a man are pure in his own eyes, but the LORD weighs the spirit" (Proverbs 16:2).

"So then each of us will give an account of himself to God" (Romans 14:12).

Perspectives from God's People

"When wealth is lost, nothing is lost; when health is lost, something is lost; when character is lost, all is lost."
—Billy Graham

"Character may be manifested in the great moments, but it is made in the small ones." —Phillips Brooks

For more: Read the blog post "Five Principles about Image and Character": epm.org/imagecharacter

Steps to Greater Happiness in Christ

The practical experience of happiness in Christ requires our sustained effort.

What steps can you take to be happier? First and foremost, by God's grace, embrace Christ's work on the cross to pay for your sins and reconcile you to God (see 2 Corinthians 5:18–21). What could be more happy-making than knowing the God of happiness, who grants us eternal life and happiness in Christ?

Once we've been reconciled to God, we can do something more about our happiness by *doing what happy people do*. Happiness doesn't precede giving and serving; it *accompanies* and *follows* it. Simply recognizing that happiness comes from knowing, loving, and serving God isn't enough. We can take an active role in our happiness by opening God's Word, going to a Bible study, joining a church, volunteering at a homeless shelter, or writing a check to support Bible translation for unreached people groups.

Insanity is doing the same things over and over while expecting different results. If we want new and better results when it comes to our happiness, we must step out and try something different.

Perspectives from God's Word

"If you look carefully into the perfect law that sets you free, and if you do what it says and don't forget what you heard, then God will bless you for doing it" (James 1:25, NLT).

"Let us use [our spiritual gifts]: . . . the one who does acts of mercy, with cheerfulness" (Romans 12:6, 8).

Perspectives from God's People

"Living for others is really the Christ life after all. Oh, the satisfaction, happiness and joy one gets out of it." —George Washington Carver

"Sacrificial service in the church doesn't start with serving. It starts with being served by God. Then as we are satisfied in Him and who He's revealed Himself to be in His crucified Son, we gladly overflow in service of others." —David Mathis

For more: Read the blog post "God's Plan for Us Includes Happiness in Him": epm.org/planhappiness

A Vastly Superior Upgrade

In every way the New Earth will be greater than the old Earth; in no sense could it ever be less.

Have you ever bought an economy ticket for a flight but because of overbooking or some other reason been upgraded to first class? Did you regret the upgrade? Did you spend your time wondering, *What am I missing out on by not being in the back of the plane?* I don't think so!

The upgrade from the old Earth to the New Earth will be vastly superior to that from economy to first class. (It may feel more like an upgrade from the baggage hold to first class.) Gone will be sin, the Curse, death, and suffering. Gone will be anything that doesn't fully reflect God's glory and creativity.

If we would miss something from our old lives and the old Earth, it would be available to us on the New Earth. Why? Because we will experience all God intends for us. He fashions us to want precisely what He will give us, so what He gives us will be exactly what we want. And since we'll be sinless, all our desires will be right and Christ-honoring.

Perspectives from God's Word

"God saw all that he had made, and it was very good" (Genesis 1:31, NIV).

"The righteous shall inherit the land and dwell upon it forever" (Psalm 37:29).

Perspectives from God's People

"Can you hear the sighing in the wind? Can you feel the heavy silence in the mountains? Can you sense the restless longing in the sea? Can you see it in the woeful eyes of an animal? Something's coming . . . something better." —Joni Eareckson Tada

"If God hath made this world so fair, where sin and death abound; how beautiful, beyond compare, will paradise be found!" —James Montgomery

For more: Read the blog post "Looking Forward to a Heaven We Can Imagine": epm.org/canimagine

You, Only Better

*On the New Earth, for the first time you'll be
the whole person God created you to be.*

God is the Creator of individual identities and personalities. He makes no two snowflakes, much less two people, alike. Not even "identical twins" are identical. Individuality preceded sin and the Curse. Individuality was God's plan from the beginning.

What makes you *you*? It's not only your body but also your memory, personality traits, gifts, passions, preferences, and interests. In the final resurrection, I believe all of these facets will be restored and amplified, untarnished by sin and the Curse.

Do you remember a time when you really felt good about yourself? Not in pride or arrogance, but when you sensed you honored God, helped the needy, were faithful, humble, and servant-hearted, like Jesus? Do you remember when you encouraged someone? When you experienced who you were meant to be? When you were running or swimming or working and felt you were strong enough to go on forever (even though later you could hardly get out of bed)? That was just a little taste of who you'll be in Heaven.

Perspectives from God's Word

"Your dead will live; their bodies will rise. You who dwell in the dust, wake up and shout for joy. . . . The earth will give birth to her dead" (Isaiah 26:19, NIV).

"I praise you, for I am fearfully and wonderfully made.
Wonderful are your works; my soul knows it very well"
(Psalm 139:14).

Perspectives from God's People

"Not the mere immortality of the soul, but rather the
resurrection of the body and the renewal of all creation
is the hope of the Christian faith." —John Piper

"This earthly Body is continually groveling on the Ground,
slow and heavy in all its Motions, listless, and soon tired
with Action; . . . but our heavenly Bodies shall be as free,
as active and nimble as our very Thoughts are." —Benjamin
Calamy

For more: Read the blog post "Will Our New Resurrection Bodies Have New
Abilities?": epm.org/newabilities

The Ultimate Family Reunion

The certainty of Heaven's ultimate reunion makes the parting bearable. The longer the separation, the more glorious the reunion.

The best part of Heaven is that we'll be with our Bridegroom, Jesus. Second best? We'll be with our family and friends who know God. That's why, when Christian loved ones die, God tells us to "not grieve like the rest who have no hope" but to comfort and "encourage one another" by anticipating the ultimate family reunion, at the greatest destination in the universe (1 Thessalonians 4:13, 18, NET).

The certainty of final, lasting reunion is so sweet that it makes the parting bearable. I don't like to be away from my family, but the one redeeming feature is the anticipation of reunion—and the longer the separation, the more glorious the reunion. In Heaven, you may meet parents you've not seen for decades or perhaps you'll meet for the first time a child (or in our case a grandchild) who died before birth.

Some have said there will be no such thing as family in Heaven. On the contrary, there will be one great family, and none of us will ever be left out. Every time we see someone, it will be a family reunion.

Perspectives from God's Word

"We do not want you to be uninformed, brothers, about those who are asleep, that you may not grieve as others do who have no hope" (1 Thessalonians 4:13).

"Jesus said, 'Truly, I say to you, there is no one who has left house or brothers or sisters or mother or father or children or lands, for my sake and for the gospel, who will not receive a hundredfold now in this time, houses and brothers and sisters and mothers and children and lands, with persecutions, and in the age to come eternal life'" (Mark 10:29–30).

Perspectives from God's People

"If we know our loved ones down here on earth, undoubtedly we shall know them more completely up there, in a most profound fellowship of love." —Steven Waterhouse

"The joys we find in the companionship of noble, unselfish, thoughtful people here give only the faintest conception of the joys of heaven's companionships." —R. A. Torrey

For more: Read the blog post "Does It Dishonor God for Us to Long for Reunion with Loved Ones?": epm.org/reunion

The Gift of Truth

*Truth matters because it is bigger
than we are. God's Word is the
truth that sets us free.*

The greatest kindness we can offer one another is the truth. Our job is not just to help each other feel good but to help each other be good. We often seem to think that our only options are to (1) speak the truth hurtfully, or (2) remain silent in the name of grace. Both are lies. The answer isn't grace *or* truth, but grace *and* truth. Jesus came full of both (see John 1:14).

Aleksandr Solzhenitsyn said in his Nobel Prize acceptance address, "One word of truth shall outweigh the entire world."[14] What did he mean? That the truth is bigger than we are. Just as the Berlin Wall finally toppled, the weight of all the world's lies can be toppled by a single truth. Truth resonates in the human heart. People may resist it, yet it's the truth they need, for it's the truth that sets them free.

God promises, "[My word] will not return to me empty, but will accomplish what I desire and achieve the purpose for which I sent it" (Isaiah 55:11, NIV). As you go through life, don't let your feelings—real as they are—invalidate your need to let the truth of God's words guide your thinking. Remember that the path to your heart travels through your mind. Truth matters.

Perspectives from God's Word

"You will know the truth, and the truth will set you free" (John 8:32).

"Sanctify them in the truth; your word is truth" (John 17:17).

Perspectives from God's People

"Christ's people . . . must have bold, unflinching, lion-like hearts, loving Christ first, and His truth next, and Christ and His truth beyond all the world." —Charles Spurgeon

"A man who loves you the most is the man who tells you the most truth about yourself." —Robert Murray M'Cheyne

For more: Read the blog post "Speak the Truth in Love": epm.org/truthlove

Under Grace, Not Sin

God's grace is His giving to us, at great cost, the goodness we don't deserve.

S in always has been and always will be irrational. It seems to make sense for the moment, but it lacks all perspective and denies reality so that truth eventually catches up with it. Scripture tells us, "Nothing in all creation is hidden from God. Everything is naked and exposed before his eyes, and he is the one to whom we are accountable" (Hebrews 4:13, NLT). God warns us that "you may be sure that your sin will find you out" (Numbers 32:23, NIV).

While the Christian life is certainly fraught with temptations and struggles, Christ's work on our behalf is sufficient to give us victory over sin so it does not master us. We are not "under sin" or "under law," but we are still under something, something unbelievably wonderful: *grace.* "For sin shall not be master over you, for you are not under law but under grace" (Romans 6:14, NASB).

If we believe that "God is for us" (Romans 8:31), then even when Scripture exposes our sin, we still trust Him, because He desires to meet and defang our sin with His forgiving and empowering grace.

Perspectives from God's Word

"See if there be any grievous way in me, and lead me in the way everlasting!" (Psalm 139:24).

"I acknowledged my sin to you, and I did not cover my iniquity; I said, 'I will confess my transgressions to the Lord,' and you forgave the iniquity of my sin" (Psalm 32:5).

Perspectives from God's People

"Sin is the mouthiest of backseat drivers, the one who, as often as we allow it, hurtles over our shoulder, elbows us in the face, and grabs for the steering wheel." —Jonathan Parnell

"Sin is treason, not sinus trouble. God forgives sin; he does not heal sin." —Rosaria Butterfield

For more: Read the article "When It Comes to Living the Christian Life, Where Do Our Efforts Come In?": epm.org/efforts

The Fountain of Living Waters

May we recognize that our deepest longings and needs can only be fulfilled by God Himself.

The world is full of desperate people thirsting for happiness. What they long for and desperately need can be found solely in the one and only "fountain of living waters": God Himself. God laments over the poor choices we make: "My people have committed two evils: they have forsaken me, the fountain of living waters, and hewed out cisterns for themselves, broken cisterns that can hold no water" (Jeremiah 2:13).

I find God to be pure, refreshing, and satisfying. My happiest days are those in which I drink most deeply of Him. I also know that if I don't drink of Him, I will drink something else—something that will leave me thirsty, dissatisfied, and sick. For idols cannot satisfy. George Whitefield wrote, "I drank of God's Pleasure as out of a River. *Oh that all were made Partakers of this living Water.*"[15]

Are you thirsty for happiness, for meaning, peace, contentment? Jesus invites you to join millions throughout history and across the globe, and a multitude of those now living in the visible presence of the fountain of living waters, to come to Him and drink the best water in the universe, the only refreshment that will ever truly and eternally satisfy.

Perspectives from God's Word

"O Lord, the hope of Israel, all who forsake you shall be put
to shame; those who turn away from you shall be written in
the earth, for they have forsaken the Lord, the fountain of
living water" (Jeremiah 17:13).

"Jesus said to her, 'Everyone who drinks of this water will be
thirsty again, but whoever drinks of the water that I will give
him will never be thirsty again. The water that I will give him
will become in him a spring of water welling up to eternal
life'" (John 4:13–14).

Perspectives from God's People

"The soul's deepest thirst is for God himself, who has
made us so that we can never be satisfied without him."
—F. F. Bruce

"We too often try to quench our thirst from pools of muddy
water when our shepherd always leads us to fresh, still
waters." —Burk Parsons

For more: Read the blog post "Are You Looking for Satisfaction in All the
Wrong Places?": epm.org/satisfaction

Dependence and the Heart of Prayer

*I ask God to help me see prayer as an adventure,
coming into His presence and beholding Him.*

The more conscious our dependence on Christ, the more we will pray without ceasing and obey Scripture's command to "pray in the Spirit on all occasions with all kinds of prayers and requests" (Ephesians 6:18, NIV).

I ask God to help me see prayer as an adventure in which I come into His presence and behold Him, and become so absorbed with Him that I don't want to do anything else. I've tasted that level of intimacy, but I long for more.

I often think about how magnificent it will be to live on the New Earth as a resurrected being, to see God's face, to consciously delight in everything around me as a direct extension of God's magnificence. I'll be delivered from my sin-tainted self and fully free to be the Christ-empowered righteous self that God designed me to be, in continual, conscious recognition of Him. This is at the heart of prayer. Let's ask God to help us taste that now, in every prayer, short or long, throughout our days.

Perspectives from God's Word

"Continue steadfastly in prayer, being watchful in it with thanksgiving" (Colossians 4:2).

"Rising very early in the morning, while it was still dark, [Jesus] departed and went out to a desolate place, and there he prayed" (Mark 1:35).

Perspectives from God's People

"Prayer is beyond any question the highest activity of the human soul. Man is at his greatest and highest when, upon his knees, he comes face to face with God." —D. Martyn Lloyd-Jones

"Prayer does not fit us for the greater work; prayer *is* the greater work." —Oswald Chambers

For more: Read the blog post "Prayer, Dependence, and Our Unhindered Access to God's Throne": epm.org/accessthrone

Cultivating
God-Consciousness

*True happiness in God is found when
we take time to develop a real
one-to-one relationship with Him.*

The simple, daily cultivation of God-consciousness has had a central role in the increasing happiness I've experienced over the years. I often have coffee with God, and sometimes I have a meal alone with Him. Occasionally when I'm praying, and those who've read my novel *Safely Home* may relate to this, I pull out a chair for Jesus and envision Him occupying it. (Not only did He sit in chairs, He also built them!) I talk to Him and listen for His voice, asking Him to speak both through His Word and His Spirit.

I'm not *pretending* Jesus is with me at lunch or when I pray; I simply believe His promise that He *really is* with me and I act in keeping with it. If you want to be happy, put meaning to the sometimes-empty phrase "spending time with God."

We can't spend time with many of the world's famous people, but I have a hunch we'd often be disappointed if we could. We can, however, spend time with God daily, hour by hour. To do so is not an impossible chore but an ongoing delight that will never disappoint. Yes, sometimes we will be more aware of His presence than at other times, but when we remind ourselves He is with us always, and He even indwells us, we'll be amazed at His love.

Perspectives from God's Word

"I pray that out of his glorious riches he may strengthen you with power through his Spirit in your inner being, so that Christ may dwell in your hearts through faith" (Ephesians 3:16–17, NIV).

"Surely I am with you always, to the very end of the age" (Matthew 28:20, NIV).

Perspectives from God's People

"When alone with God, be alone with Him. Begin in silence. Speak with simplicity. Listen in meekness. Never leave without a conscious season of real communion." —Samuel Chadwick

"I bear my testimony . . . that there is no joy to be found in all this world like that of sweet communion with Christ!" —Charles Spurgeon

For more: Read the blog post "The Simple, Daily Cultivation of God-Consciousness": epm.org/simplecultivation

Empowered
for Holiness

*To be holy in Christ's strength
and for His glory: that's our
calling and our joy.*

D on't forget that "the one [Christ] who is in you is greater than the one who is in the world" (1 John 4:4, NIV). As powerful as the evil one is to tempt us, God is infinitely more powerful to deliver us and has in Christ given us all the resources we need to live godly lives.

In Leviticus, God repeatedly tells His people to be holy because He is holy (see, for example, 11:45; 19:2; 20:26).

God is the reason we should be holy. But He's also the empowerment for our holiness. Many of us are convinced we should be more holy, but we've gone about it wrong. To be holy in our strength, and for our glory, is to be distinctly unholy. To be holy in Christ's strength and for His glory: that's our calling and our joy.

Christ intercedes for us (see Romans 8:34) for the same reason we intercede for one another: we need help, and we need God's power to resist temptation and live holy lives. Since the prayers of a righteous man are "effective" (James 5:16, NIV), what could be more effective than Christ's prayers for us? What an encouragement to know that even if no one else knows our needs and is praying for us, Christ does and is.

Perspectives from God's Word

"The grace of God has appeared, bringing salvation for all people, training us to renounce ungodliness and worldly passions, and to live self-controlled, upright, and godly lives in the present age" (Titus 2:11–12).

"His divine power has granted to us all things that pertain to life and godliness" (2 Peter 1:3).

Perspectives from God's People

"The Spirit's work is not to make us holy, in order that we may be pardoned, but to show us the cross, where the pardon is to be found by the unholy; so that having found the pardon there, we may begin the life of holiness to which we are called." —Horatius Bonar

"Lord, make me as holy as a pardoned sinner can be made." —Robert Murray M'Cheyne

For more: Read the blog post "Should God's People Want to Be Both Holy and Happy?": epm.org/happyholy

Living for the Life to Come

This life is your opportunity to invest in the next.

How do you want to be remembered? As a man or woman who walked intimately with God and obeyed Him, who spent life not pursuing treasures on Earth but treasures in Heaven? As a wife who faithfully served God through serving her family? As a husband who loved and nurtured his wife and his children? As a follower of Christ intimately familiar with the Scriptures, who lived out God's Word, who delighted in telling others of His love and grace? Now let me ask: What are you doing to make people remember you in such a way?

Has your life left you unprepared to face death? Be encouraged! You're still alive, and life means opportunity. *Today* you can change the course of your life, to God's glory. And, best of all, if you know Jesus, He promises you will live forever: "Whoever hears my word and believes him who sent me has eternal life" (John 5:24).

This life is your opportunity; that's why it is such a shame to waste it on fame, fortune, self-pity, anxiety, and resentment. Choose to invest it in God, in His people, in His kingdom program. Outlive your life by investing it in eternity!

Perspectives from God's Word

"O Lord, make me know my end and what is the measure of my days; let me know how fleeting I am!" (Psalm 39:4).

"[Jesus said,] 'I glorified you [, Father,] on earth, having accomplished the work that you gave me to do'" (John 17:4).

Perspectives from God's People

"It ought to be the business of every day, to prepare for our last day." —Matthew Henry

"Soon you will read in the newspaper that I am dead. Don't believe it for a moment. I will be more alive than ever before. . . . Earth recedes. . . . Heaven opens before me!" —D. L. Moody

For more: Read the blog post "Outlive Your Life": epm.org/outlivelife

About the Author

Randy Alcorn is an author and the director of Eternal Perspective Ministries (EPM), a nonprofit ministry dedicated to teaching principles of God's Word and assisting the church in ministering to the unreached, unfed, unborn, untrained, unreconciled, and unsupported people around the world. His ministry focus is communicating the strategic importance of using our earthly time, money, possessions, and opportunities to invest in need-meeting ministries that count for eternity. He accomplishes this by analyzing, teaching, and applying biblical truth.

Before starting EPM in 1990, Randy served as a pastor for fourteen years. He holds degrees in theology and biblical studies and has taught on the adjunct faculties of Multnomah University and Western Seminary, both in Portland, Oregon.

Randy is the best-selling author of over fifty books (over ten million sold), including the novels *Deadline, Dominion,* and *Deception* as well as *Edge of Eternity, The Chasm, Safely Home,* and *Courageous.* His nonfiction works include *Heaven; If God Is Good; Managing God's Money; Money, Possessions, and Eternity; The Treasure Principle; The Grace and Truth Paradox; 60 Days of Happiness;* and *The Law of Rewards.* Randy has written for many magazines and produces the popular magazine *Eternal Perspectives.* He's been a guest on numerous radio and television programs, including *Focus on the Family, The Bible Answer Man, Family Life Today,* and *Revive Our Hearts.*

The father of two married daughters, Karina and Angela, Randy lives in Gresham, Oregon, with Nanci, his wife and best friend, and their golden retriever, Maggie. They are the proud grandparents of Jake, Matt, Ty, Jack, and David. Randy enjoys hanging out with his family, biking, underwater photography, research, and reading.

Connect with Randy online

Facebook: facebook.com/randyalcorn

Twitter: twitter.com/randyalcorn

Pinterest: pinterest.com/randyalcorn

Blog: epm.org/blog

To view a full list of Randy's books, visit epm.org/books.

About Eternal
Perspective Ministries

Eternal Perspective Ministries (EPM) is a Bible-believing, Christ-centered nonprofit organization with two goals:

- To teach the principles of God's Word, emphasizing an eternal viewpoint;
- To reach the needy in Christ's name, calling attention to the needs of the unreached, unfed, unsupported, unborn, unreconciled, and untrained.

One hundred percent of the royalties from Randy's books go to Christian ministries. So God uses Randy's books to change people's lives in two ways: through the reading of his words and through the giving away of his royalties. Since its inception in 1990, EPM has contributed $8 million in book royalties to ministries around the world.

You can order all of Randy's books and products through EPM's online store at epm.org. (The EPM website also has many free resources, including articles, audio, video, pastors' kits, and more.) When you purchase Randy's books from EPM, the profits go directly to support the work of the ministry and fund EPM's operating expenses.

EPM produces *Eternal Perspectives,* a free magazine filled with thought-provoking and informative articles, most authored by Randy, on a variety of subjects related to Christian living, Heaven, giving, missions, and much more. EPM also sends weekly e-mail updates with the latest about Randy's books, projects, and speaking events, as well as featured family news and special promotions from EPM. You can subscribe to both at epm.org/subscribe.

Contact Eternal Perspective Ministries online at epm.org or at 39085 Pioneer Boulevard, Suite 206, Sandy, OR 97055, or by phone at 503-668-5200 or toll free 1-877-376-4567.

Connect with Eternal Perspective Ministries

Facebook: facebook.com/EPMinistries

Twitter: twitter.com/epmorg

Vimeo: vimeo.com/randyalcorn/videos

Instagram: instagram.com/randyalcorn_epm

Blog: epm.org/resources/

Notes

1. Day 9: *The Autobiography of Charles H. Spurgeon,* ed. Susannah Spurgeon and Joseph Harrold (Cincinnati: Curtis and Jennings, 1898), 1:76.
2. Day 12: Colin S. Smith, *The Plan* (Wheaton, IL: Crossway, 2011), 20.
3. Day 14: C. S. Lewis, *"The Weight of Glory": and Other Addresses* (New York: HarperCollins, 2001), 182.
4. Day 15: Joni Eareckson Tada, *Glorious Intruder: God's Presence in Life's Chaos* (Colorado Springs: Multnomah, 1989), 25.
5. Day 21: John D. Rockefeller, quoted in *The Speaker's Quote Book,* comp. Roy B. Zuck (Grand Rapids, MI: Kregel, 1997), 260.
6. Day 35: John Chrysostom, *Six Books on the Priesthood,* trans. Graham Neville (London: SPCK, 1964), 130.
7. Day 37: K. Connie Kang, "Next Stop, the Pearly Gates . . . ," *Los Angeles Times,* October 24, 2003, http://articles.latimes.com/2003/oct/24/nation/na-heaven24.
8. Day 56: "Do the Next Thing," quoted in *The Elisabeth Elliot Newsletter,* July/August 1994, www.elisabethelliot.org/newsletters/july-aug-94.pdf.

9. Day 59: Sinclair Ferguson, *In Christ Alone: Living the Gospel-Centered Life* (Lake Mary, FL: Reformation Trust, 2007), 190.

10. Day 64: Lewis Smedes, *The Art of Forgiving: When You Need to Forgive and Don't Know How* (New York: Ballantine, 1997), 178.

11. Day 69: *Saint Augustine's Confessions* (Lafayette, IN: Sovereign Grace, 2001), 1.

12. Day 71: C. S. Lewis, *Christian Behaviour,* in *Mere Christianity,* in *The Complete C. S. Lewis Signature Classics* (New York: HarperCollins, 2001), 128.

13. Timothy Keller, *The Freedom of Self-Forgetfulness* (Leyland, England: 10 Publishing, 2012), 32–33.

14. Day 84: Aleksandr Solzhenitsyn, in *Nobel Lectures, Literature 1968–1980,* ed. Sture Allén (Singapore: World Scientific, 1993), www.nobelprize.org/nobel_prizes/literature /laureates/1970/solzhenitsyn-lecture.html.

15. Day 86: George Whitefield, *A Continuation of the Reverend Mr. Whitefield's Journal* (London: Strahan, 1741), Journal 7:28, italics in the original.

Other Books from Randy Alcorn

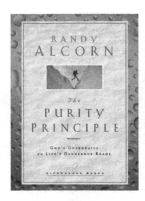

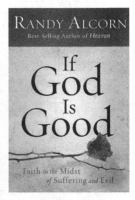

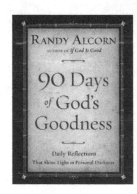

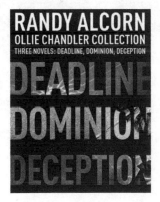

Randy Alcorn Reveals the Secret of Joyful Giving in this All-New Video Curriculum!

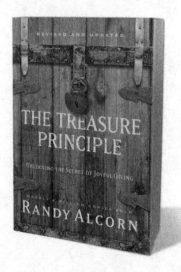 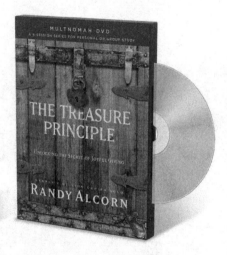

Now you can experience Randy Alcorn's transformative teaching on this concept through this all-new video curriculum. Through four sessions, ideal for small group or church use, he explores the guidelines and rewards of giving as highlighted in the six "Treasure Principle Keys" found in Scripture.

Biblical and practical, this perspective-shifting series helps Christians replace anxiety over money and possessions with something far more priceless: the liberating joy of giving!

Learn more at www.WMBooks.com/Treasure

Please enjoy a sample chapter
from Randy's book,

90 Days of God's Goodness:
Daily Reflections That Shine Light on Personal Darkness

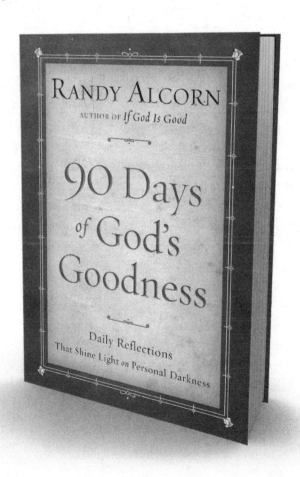

Cultivating Christlikeness

His divine power has given us everything we need for life and godliness through our knowledge of him who called us by his own glory and goodness. Through these he has given us his very great and precious promises, so that through them you may participate in the divine nature and escape the corruption in the world caused by evil desires.

For this very reason, make every effort to add to your faith goodness; and to goodness, knowledge; and to knowledge, self-control; and to self-control, perseverance; and to perseverance, godliness; and to godliness, brotherly kindness; and to brotherly kindness, love. For if you possess these qualities in increasing measure, they will keep you from being ineffective and unproductive in your knowledge of our Lord Jesus Christ....

For if you do these things, you will never fall, and you will receive a rich welcome into the eternal kingdom of our Lord and Savior Jesus Christ.

—2 PETER 1:3–8, 10–11

God has called us by his own glory and goodness and given us precious promises to help generate his character qualities in our lives. Even in severe difficulties, he is at work to make us productive followers, bearing the fruit of his Spirit.

Raised in a Christian home, Jeremy was bitter toward God because both his parents had been born with cerebral palsy. He broke his father's heart when, as a young man, Jeremy told him he would never worship a God who had done this to his parents.

Jeremy's life became a train wreck of drugs and alcohol. He went through rehabilitation centers and two separations from his wife, who prayed twenty-seven years for her husband to trust Christ.

Arrested for drunk driving, Jeremy finally broke. He yielded his life to Jesus and immediately felt the bitterness lift.

After nearly three decades of pain in her marriage, Jeremy's wife, Sarah, wrote, "I am here to tell you I would not have the relationship with God that I have if I had not suffered deeply. God revealed treasures to me that can only be found, I believe, in the darkness."

Sarah comes to the problem of evil from a distinct worldview. But there are other views. Each attempts to answer the question, "How can we reconcile evil and suffering with a God who is all-good, all-powerful, and all-knowing?" Besides the irrational conclusion that evil and suffering must not exist and the atheistic conclusion that God does not exist, the most popular ways of addressing the problem of evil minimize one or more of God's attributes, especially his power, knowledge, or goodness.

A friend wrestled with the problem of evil after a terrible accident. He concluded that we err whenever we speak of only two or three attributes of God in relation to the problem of evil. He meant that we must bring *all* of God's attributes to the table. To merely glorify and magnify God is not to make more of him than he is; that's impossible. But to stop there is to do injustice to his infinite majesty, power, wisdom, and love.

If we see God *only* in terms of his love or mercy or compassion—as wonderful as those attributes are—we will not worship the true God but an idol of our own imagination. An idol that will, in the end, disappoint us, just as everything that is not God always will.

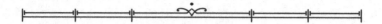

God, give us wisdom to see the world through your eyes. As you showed your servant Sarah, Jeremy's wife, show us that in our suffering you can accomplish the grand purpose of cultivating in us Christlike qualities of faith, kindness, perseverance, love, and goodness in increasing measure. Help us anticipate the rich welcome you will grant those who have submitted to your purposes to prepare us for the Person and Place we most desire.